T0078092

HONEST-SEEKING-HEARTS

JANET WHITEHEAD

authorHOUSE

AuthorHouse™
1663 Liberty Drive
Bloomington, IN 47403
www.authorhouse.com
Phone: 833-262-8899

Published by AuthorHouse 10/27/2021

ISBN: 978-1-6655-3978-4 (sc)
ISBN: 978-1-6655-3977-7 (e)

Library of Congress Control Number: 2021920250

Print information available on the last page.

The scripture quotations contained herein, unless otherwise noted are from the (
*) New American Standard Bible *, Copyright © 1960, 1971, 1977,1995, 2020
by The Lockman Foundation. Used by permission. All rights reserved.

Scripture quotations marked KJV are from the Holy Bible, King James Version
(Authorized Version). First published in 1611. Quoted from the KJV Classic
Reference Bible, Copyright © 1983 by The Zondervan Corporation.

The Message (MSG) Copyright © 1993, 2002, 2018 by Eugene H. Peterson

This book is printed on acid-free paper.

"You will seek Me and find Me when you
search for Me with all your heart."
Jeremiah 29:13

CONTENTS

DEDICATION

Words, words and more words . . . so many books have been written. As I write these words, I am sitting in the coffee shop at Barnes and Noble surrounded by thousands of books. So why am I contemplating writing one? Because I believe my Savior has spoken to my heart these words: "You cannot do this, but I can. We will partner together, and it will be a joy and a pleasure."

So, I dedicate these words to the Precious Holy Spirit whose encouragement never fails, the Father who corrects with gentle patience and the Lord Jesus, my friend.

The same voice that spoke the universe into existence, that same voice, still speaks to His children today in various ways and with the Voice comes the power to complete the task at hand.

My prayer –

Father, I relinquish my claim to myself and commend myself into Your capable hands. Amen

ACKNOWLEDGEMENTS

I want to say a special thanks to my husband Mike. You are my partner in this journey we have been on for 46 years. You have been at my side during the very hard times and the times of great joy. I love you.

To my beloved sons, Brian and Clayton, I say, "This journey we are on would not have been the same without you. Each of you are a very special gift from God."

I express my gratitude to my parents, John and Roxie Seward. They took me to church and introduced me to the Lord. Daddy's favorite bible verse was: "I sought for a man among them, that should make up the hedge, and stand in the gap before Me for the land." Ezekiel 22:30 KJV

Thank you Tom Mohn our shepherd, teacher and friend. Thank you for asking a very simple question: "What's God been saying to you lately?" That question and your willingness to listen, with sincere interest, have been a blessing to many people.

Our brother in Christ Michael Wells has gone on to be with the Lord, but his honest straightforward teaching still blesses me greatly and is woven into this book in ways I cannot even describe. One of my favorite quotes from Michael is that we Christians suffered because we do not define our words. I agreed wholeheartedly. Thank you, Betty Wells, for encouraging me to write from my heart.

Thank you Lois Crain, my sister-friend, for editing this book. Our lives are intertwined in ways only God could design. Your skill and encouragement made this publication possible.

CHAPTER 1

THE DAY THAT CHANGED MY LIFE

I would like to tell you the story of my family and the one horrific moment that changed my life forever.

My husband Mike and I were members of a church that had Friday night meetings in a home. The night I am telling you about started out like many others. There were people talking, laughing and enjoying each other before the meeting began. It's not surprising that when the phone rang I did not even notice.

Word of my parents' death had reached Mike's parents, Jim and Gerry, who managed to locate us there.

Jim told Mike that they had gone to my aunt's house in the country. My aunt and uncle were not home but when my parents arrived, they surprised a burglar who shot them dead.

Mike stood in the doorway watching me talk and laugh – his heart breaking. He told our pastor the news. Our pastor proceeded to asked me, to come into the bedroom with him, his wife Maryann and Mike. I remember smiling and thinking what a strange request. He told me to sit down on the bed while explaining why we were there. Now I know why they say, "Sit down I have something to tell you." The room went dark to me, but I did not faint. I sat in silence, my thoughts returning to a time years before when my uncle had confronted a burglar in that same house. Uncle Dell had wrestled with that man who just left quickly. We all marveled at the outcome because Uncle Dell was not a large or particularly strong man who was in his 70's. I thought Daddy would have tried to defend them, but the outcome was so different. Maryann said to me, "It's okay you can cry." But there were no tears – only stunned silence for what seemed like minutes. When we emerged from the bedroom word had spread throughout the house about their death. The people crowded around us, and I began to cry. I knew they would center their prayer that night and for some time to come on our needs. I was grateful that we were surrounded by brothers and sisters in Christ when we got the news. As we walked out into the darkness it felt heavy, like a velvet blanket. I could actually feel the presence of God. I remember later that I did not experience the stages of mourning. I went straight to acceptance. There was no denial, bargaining or anger. I guess in situations like this the only bargaining would had been "God if you get me through this then I will do something for You." There was no need of bargaining. He was so near and dear to me. As for anger, how could I be angry with One so close, so attentive and caring? He prevents and He permits things in our lives for a reason. Blessed be the name of the Lord!

When we left the meeting that night, we went to Mike's parents' house. As we came through the front door, they met us there. I said out loud what I had been wondering... "Did they suffer?" My knees slightly buckled, and my head went back but the three of them steadied me and I walked to the living room to sit down. Jim went to the kitchen to make coffee. I thought, yes Jim do something that keeps you busy – it's okay. After a few minutes Gerry said that I would need to be strong for my brother. She said that sometimes men don't cope as well at times like this. She was trying to be helpful, and I understood. But I knew in the moment that I had nothing to give. My brother would have to go to God for himself and I knew he would. We went home, packed cloths and we set out for the hospital in Muskogee. I don't remember the drive. I only remember marveling that Mike could drive and how grateful I was because I could not have done it. At the hospital there were family members and old friends. A relative had identified the bodies, another thing to be grateful for. There really was no reason to be there so we went to my brother's house to spend a very fitful and restless night. Crying hard and long lead to moments of sleep interrupted by violent jerks of the whole body. Years later during a routine physical exam including an EKG I was told that it showed an old infarction, but my heart was otherwise strong. I know it happened that night. Emotional pain and physical pain cannot be separated.

The next day we rose and cried and looked at each other. Sorrow met sorrow; hearts began to mend. Johnny, my nephew, sat beside me on the couch. He held my hand.

There were the days that followed. The choosing of caskets, the visitation for close family. I will not belabor those details. Suffice to say, it was hard and painful, but we were together, and God's comfort was ever present.

I had just received the worst news of my life, but God in His infinite mercy knew that wonderful news was on the horizon. A few weeks later I was told that I was pregnant. Precious lives were taken away. But Brian, our first born, was growing inside me. He was the child of my mourning.

The funeral attendance was huge. My parents had lived in Muskogee a very long time and the circumstances called out for attention.

The man who had killed them had been caught within hours of the crime. He was driving erratically and was in possession of things belonging to my aunt. He was charged with murder and jailed in Muskogee. At one point he escaped jail, killed one more person and left one for dead before he was captured again. When I heard that he had escaped I remember having the irrational fear that he would come after my brother or me. The feeling pasted in about a day. I just kept praying that he would be caught again and that the trial would be over before my baby was born. As God would have it, my request was granted. The trial did happen, and the conviction was handed down in September. He spent years appealing the conviction and was eventually executed.

On the way to the funeral, I remember thinking that Mom and Dad were in heaven. I thought that their murderer would be forgiven if he repented and cried out to God for forgiveness. I could imagine Daddy smiling and reaching out to shake his hand when he entered heaven. If that was meant to be, God would have to bring it about. I do not know if it happened but, I do know that their church was turned upside down. John and Roxie gone – murdered! It shook them to the core. The pastor retired and a new pastor came. All these years later I do not know the spiritual condition of that church but for some years after their death it come to life. Praise God!

I wish I could say that I lived every day with the peace of God but that would not be the truth. As the years passed It was fear that came to be my constant companion. The more you have to lose the more fear can grip you. In 1984 Clayton was born; another precious child and more to lose.

I am grateful to Ann Voscamp for helping me see the truth about my fear of loss. She helped me see that gratitude to God for everything I do have builds faith. Fear destroys it. It is, after all, His peace that He so graciously offers us. It is His perfect peace that casts out all fear.

"My peace I leave with you; My peace I give to you; not as the world gives do I give to you. Do not let your heart be troubles, nor let it be fearful." John 14:27

"There is no fear in love; but perfect love casts out fear, because fear involves punishment and the one who fears is not perfected in love." 1 John 4:18

I don't mean to convey the idea that I understand it all. But embracing the mystery of life is a better way to live.

Father God did not spare His own Son but gave Him up for us all. Why did I grow to distrust Him so? I think it was because I stopped living in the moment. When they died, I had no strength to think about the future or the past. Nothing would change the reality – the finality of death.

Someone said, "Wherever you are – be all there." It's easier said than done. It takes practice and determination.

The only place I can love Him is here and now. "Perfect love casts out fear." God's love is perfect. Mine is flawed but growing.

I never really asked the question, "Why me? Why my family?"

The real question is why we are lavished upon by such a great God? Why does He put up with our ingratitude and our wanting more and more?

I am in His debt. He is not in my debt. There are gifts in everything, even things I do not like or understand.

Psalm 8:4-5,9 "What is man, that Thou dost take thought of him? And the son of man, that Thou dost care for him? Yet Thou hast made him a little lower than God, and dost crown him with glory and majesty! O Lord, our Lord, how majestic is Thy name in all the earth!"

Precious Memories

My parents were not just victims of a violent crime that took their lives. They were real people with hopes and dreams.

"The righteous people we have known will be remembered for a long time and those who remember them will be blessed." (My paraphrase) Proverbs 112:6 and Proverbs 10:7

I would like to share with you some of the precious memories of my parents and my life since their passing. I hope these memories will bless you the reader of this book.

I grew up living in the country a few miles outside Muskogee. My mother, Roxie Seward, was 36 years old and my father was 40 when I was born. My only sibling, Claybourn is fifteen years older than me. Suffice to say I was a surprise. In fact, my mother was concerned that she might have cancer and relieved to find out it was me instead. My dad's name is John which means God is Gracious. I'm sure they did not know that. Nor did they know that my name, Janet, comes from the name John. After waiting several years I would like to think they thought of me as God's gift to them.

Daddy was a factory worker, a farmer and a cattleman. It was farming that he loved. My brother, Claybourn, lived nearby and they farmed the land together. My mother was a home maker, an excellent cook and a seamstress. She made most of my cloths and her own also. To this day, over forty years later, when I go in a fabric shop for some small item, I think of her, and I miss her. My love of fashion was a result of our collaborative efforts. I designed my cloths and she loved sewing them for me.

When I was a child there were no neighbors with children near my home, but I didn't seem to mind. I had my beagle puppies, chicken eggs to gather and an imagination. I spent much of my time outdoors enjoying country life.

We went to church faithfully. Daddy was a Sunday School Superintendent and a deacon. Momma worked in the office and the church nursery. I enjoyed the sermons. It gave me a chance to listen and learn. I'm sure I didn't understand a lot, but many truths were planted in my mind that would bless me all my life.

I was about nine years old when I felt the conviction of the sin in my life, walked the isle at the end of the service and accepted Jesus as my savior. I had never heard the words "age of accountability", but I actually know the exact moment I arrived at that age. I was at school one day enjoying recess by running and playing on the playground behind Jefferson Elementary School. Children were running, yelling and having fun. It was a pretty noisy place to be when a child ran up to me and asked which direction another child had gone. In that moment I lied. I told that child the exact opposite direction. Then a very important thing happened. I stood very still as I was lost in thought. The reality of my sin hit home to me. It was as though the playground went silent. I probably closed my eyes because I didn't see all the commotion. I can't say I heard a voice, but I did have a clear realization that what I had done was wrong. I was a sinner! The emotion of shame is a gift from God. It gives us the opportunity to repent. Soon after this revelation I gave my life to Jesus, and I have never doubted my salvation.

Not long after my conversion we got the news that a family friend was getting a divorce. I really did not understand the complexities of married life, but I remember thinking that they should have prayed before they married. Then one day when I was walking in the front yard and standing under the mimosa tree. I prayed that God would send the man He had for me to marry. As the years went by, I often recalled that prayer and God in His mercy sent me the love of my life, my husband Mike.

Daddy was a very outgoing man. He never met a stranger. When the garden produced more food than my mother could preserve by either freezing and canning, he would put it in the back of the pickup, drive to an intersection that had space to park, and sell the produce. He called it "truck farming." I think he did it as much for the fun of it as the money.

My mother was shyer and more reserved than my dad but very sweet and personable. Once there was a young child that she took care of in the church nursery who named their new puppy Roxie because he loved my mother so much. She thought it was funny and sweet. One of her sayings was "Every momma cow thinks her baby calf is the prettiest." That saying is a country way of describing the partiality all mothers show to their own. My brother's children had the privilege of knowing my parents well. They lived most of their childhood on the farm in their home very close to my parents. My children, Brian and Clayton never met their grandparents. I accept the fact of God's permissive will. I bow to His Sovereignty but, of course I wish my sons could have known them.

I wasn't surprised by the love I felt for our two sons. I had nine months to adjust to the idea of being a mother, but each time our son Brian and our daughter-in-law Lauren called from Iowa to give us the news that she was going to have a baby I was completely shocked at the depth of love I had for an unborn child. I thought my love would happen as I had a chance to meet each one and develop a relationship. But it is as if I knew Robin and Holly before they were born. I think we are more connected to other human beings than we realize, especially family. It is as if an invisible connective tissue comes into play, and we can know others on a spiritual level that transcends distance and time.

There is a depth of love God has for us that we cannot comprehend.
He has known us from all eternity past.

There is an old hymn that puts it this way:
He loved me before I knew Him, and all my love is due Him. He plunged me to victory beneath the crimson flood. That crimson flood refers to the blood of Jesus that was shed for us. Life is in the blood.

There are sweet children everywhere but, the blood line matters. How sweet of our Heavenly Father to adopt us into the holy blood line, and plunge/baptize us into His eternal family.

Ephesians 1:5 He predestined us to adoption as sons through Jesus Christ to Himself, according to the kind intentions of his will.

I don't mean to paint a picture of my childhood as being totally idyllic. We were not wealthy, but all our needs were met. As I said before my father was a very friendly person, but he mostly left my upbringing to my mother. We were not as close as we could have been. After I got married at twenty-two years old, I began to seek God in a more personal way. As

I drew near to God, He began to remind me of little things my father had said or done that offended me when I was a child. When I recounted them to my husband each offence seemed small and petty. I heard God speak these words to my mind, He said; "If you want to get closer to your Heavenly Father you must deal with the relationship you have with your earthly father." God's gentle but direct words of rebuke inspired me to reach out to my dad. I did not confront him about anything. I just reached out in a tender way, and he responded beautifully. I am very grateful this happened because within about three years his spirit had departed this world. The times we shared before he was gone to be with the Lord are precious memories. The hymn Precious Memories expresses my sentiments beautifully.

J.B.F Wright lyrics

Precious memories how they linger.
How they ever flood my soul.
In the stillness of the midnight,
Precious sacred scenes unfold.

I would like to share another precious memory from about ten years ago. It was midday in the summertime, and I was outdoors. The insect called locust were chirping their summertime sounds. The combination of heat, lack of breeze and the sound of locust reminded me of hot summer days on the farm. What happened next was similar to a vision or an out of body experience. In my mind I was standing on the dirt road that led from our house to the barn. On my right was the soybean silo, on my left was the older of the two barns and I could hear the locust singing their song. The next thing that happened was amazing. These lyrics and the lilting tune of an old folk song came to my mind.

It was good to be young then, to be close to the earth.
Now the green leaves of summer are calling me home.

This mental/spiritual trip home only lasted long enough to see the sights and hear the words, but it is now a precious memory that floods my soul with calmness and peace.

**Precious father, loving mother, Fly across the lonely years;
And old home scenes of my childhood, In fond memory appears.**

The apostle Paul told us; "Whatever is true, whatever is honorable (worthy of respect), whatever is right. Whatever is pure, whatever is lovely, whatever is of good repute, if there is any excellence and anything worthy of praise, let your mind dwell on these things." Ephesians 4:8

These lovely things could be in the present and they could be memories from our past.

Precious Loving Heavenly Father I come to You. As I grow older and travel through this journey, called life with You, I realize more and more that your hand has been on me all the time. Your providential will includes me and I am awe struck. I realize that your plan for your chosen ones is filled with challenges, painful moments and with joy unspeakable and full of glory.

As I travel on life's pathway, Know now what the years may hold;

As I study your prophetic plan for the ages I realize we are living in the time of your return. I recall to my mind your tender mercies and I am grateful to be counted among those who will spend eternity with you. Amen

As I ponder, hope grows fonder. Precious memories flood my soul.

CHAPER 2

INNOCENCE LOST – INNOCENCE SHATTERED

In literature characters lose their innocence when they discover that there are things in life that are not fair. Injustice does happen to themselves and to those they love. They are confronted by evil, and they are required to react. Innocence in this context does not mean sinless. It means untested.

On February 09, 1979 I faced a circumstance that tested my faith in God. He was faithful to carry me through the crisis and He has been faithful to this very day.

I used to have a sense of adventure and optimism. But after my parents were murdered when I was 27 years old, something changed in me. God's loving care during that time of mourning was nothing short of miraculous and I will be eternally grateful to the Lord my redeemer and His Spirit my comforter. However, the enemy did creep in and take advantage of my shattered innocence. Emotionally I felt the need to brace myself against the inevitable shock of loss and pain. When my sons were children, I did not mention to them that their grandparents had died a violent death. It was hard to know when they were old enough and the time just never seemed right. In 2013, some 34 years after they died, I felt God encourage me to write out my memories of the event in the form of a letter and give it to them both. I now feel a similar nudge and that is why I shared those very personal words with you in this book.

> May God receive the glory He deserves, and
> may you the reader be blessed.
> I pray we all learn to live moment by moment
> and **experience** the presence.
> of our Lord and Savior Jesus Christ. Amen

THE JOURNEY BEGINS

In the years since their passing, my life has been a journey of discovering who God really is and, in the process, I've learned a lot about myself. In the following pages I would like to share with you my personal experience with God's power found, God's power lost and found again. I want to be very clear about one thing. I do not believe we lose our salvation when we sin as believers. But as the old song says, we are prone to wander from the One we love.

In His mercy He even redeems our wanderings, and He uses the valuable lessons we learn to bless ourselves and others. The process God set in motion is still going on to this day.

"Lord – Indwelling Spirit, I praise You! The plan that includes me and Your chosen others is an incredible plan, full of tender mercies. I repent of coming to believe You were not kind and tender toward us. I pictured Your mercies as severe, harsh and reluctant. How wrong of me! How unfair! Holy Spirit . . . I realize that I use the name <u>Lord</u> because I am more comfortable with a less specific name. Father . . . not a name I use often. Intimacy is what You want – I want it too. Help me Lord Jesus, Father God, Spirit of Holiness. How do I talk to the Triune Spirit within me? I hear You say, "HONESTLY."

"Dear God, I need You."

"As I listen You remind me of the words or a hymn; "Love Divine – All Love Excelling." Only Your love is divine. My love is flawed, selfish and mixed with human weakness. But it is true love when I abide in You. Your love is excellent and pure." Amen

<u>My Utmost for His Highest</u> by Oswald Chamber APRIL 30TH an amazing parallel to my prayer.

"Love suffereth long, and is kind . . . "1 Cor. 8:4-8 KJV

Oswald Chambers said, "The springs of love are in God, not in us. It is absurd to look for the love of God in our hearts naturally, it is only there when it has been shed abroad in our hearts by the Holy Spirit."

God was beginning to reveal to me just how
far I had wandered from His love.

A revelation is a thought of supernatural origin.

**It is for the purpose of unsealing or unveiling hidden
truths at the exact moment of His choosing.**

I have decided to record an event that happened many years ago. It seemed to have some significance at the time but grows for me with each passing year.

Clayton was about six or seven years old. I am approaching forty and questioning my purpose in life. Wife, mother, teacher are all words that describe and define things I do, but not who I am. There seemed to be something else. This particular night Clayton was upset by something that had happened that day. As I leaned over him in bed for one last hug I was reminded of words from the book of Esther. Mordecai spoke to Esther and said. "Perhaps it was for such a time as this that you were born." I questioned God. Could my whole purpose in life be fulfilled in one act of mothering? These words were puzzling. I even questioned if God had spoken them to me at all. As time went by and in the days that followed, He did use those very words to reveal my calling.

Esther's parents were dead. She had been adopted by her uncle Mordecai. Through a series of events, she became the queen of the nation in which her kinsmen were exiled. Haman, an enemy of the Jews plotted their annihilation. She prayed, fasted and took action. She went in before the Persian king Ahasuerus without having been invited which could have had grave consequences. But through prayer and fasting God used her to spare her people. She could have died because of her actions. But she survived and so did they.

So . . . What does this story have to do with me?

God was calling me to fast and pray for my little kingdom, my kin, my family. As I am faithful to die to myself, seek the King of Glory's face and learn to know Him, God has been faithful to get the "wrong one out" (my flesh represented by Haman) and to get the "right one in" (the Holy Spirit represented by Mordecai.) He will fulfill His promise to spare us from spiritual separation from God.

> The deepest longing of my heart, in relation to my family
> is to converse on a deep level about the God we all love.
> As our family has grown larger that longing has grown even stronger.

AS GOD CONTINUES THIS JOURNEY WITH ME, HE IS GIVING ME A CLARITY I HAVE LONGED FOR.

God had already revealed to me that focusing too much on how God works – the steps and outcome can lead to trying to predict the future. And that these thought patterns taken too far are forms of superstition, sentimentalism and are the product of unfulfilled emotions.

The desire to know what tragedy was just around the corner and the desire to brace myself for it had taken me down a very dark road. But God in His mercy was not through with me yet. In the days, weeks and months that followed He spoke to me of my real identity as a partner of the King and the call to intercede for my family. God exposed my coping mechanisms, in other words, my idols.

In Psalms 119:79 David does not encourage his people to turn to himself because he is their savior. He encourages them to turn to him because he is confident that turning to him will direct them away from idols and toward the saving grace of God.

> "May those who (reverently and worshipfully) fear Thee turn to me,
> Even those who know Thy testimonies." (descriptive words added)

He longs for those who will join him in reverently worshiping God; those who have known God's word to be trustworthy and are willing to lay aside their idols of presumption and superstition.

As God would have it, a quote from Thomas Manton (1620-1677) confirmed that truth and prepared me for more intense revelation.

"Fear and knowledge make up a godly person. Knowledge without fear breeds presumption. Fear without knowledge breeds superstition. Blind zeal, like a blind horse, may be full of spirit, but it is always stumbling. Knowledge must direct fear, and fear must season knowledge; then it is a happy mixture and composition."

If fear of the Lord is the beginning of wisdom, and it is because the Bible says it is, then my fear was seriously misplaced. As I would read years later in the book <u>1000 Gifts,</u> the result of my focusing on loss was ungratefulness. I prefer to think of fear as a symptom of unbelief like a fever is a symptom of an infection. I had allowed myself to be infected with the disease of sinful ingratitude.

The next milestone in my journey came when I opened the book <u>Still Higher for His Highest</u> (sequel to <u>My Utmost for His Highest</u>) by Oswald Chambers. I opened it randomly, as I often do, and my eyes fell on the words of February 18. I began to read. He described me to a tee. It hurt to read this and felt strangely good at the same time.

The Snare of the Sentimentalist
Luke 9:57, 62

"Lord, I will follow Thee, but . . . "The wish ought to be followed by immediate obedience. I must take the wish and translate it into resolution and then into action. If I do not, the wish will translate into a corrupting instead of a redeeming power in my life. .... Consequently, a sentimentalist is usually callous, <u>self-centered</u> and <u>selfish,</u> because the emotions he likes to have stirred do not usually cost us anything."

Sentimentality defined is exaggerated <u>self-indulgent</u> tenderness, sadness, and reliance on feelings as a guide.

We sentimentalist are always wishing and hoping for the best while anticipating the worst. Immediate obedience would mean saying," Lord, I will risk dying to myself and suffering if it is Your plan for my life. You know best and I denounce the emotional prison I have gotten used to and I denounce the habit of trying to anticipate the future."

Those unfulfilled emotions lead us around and around in circles. "Always learning and never able to come to the knowledge of the truth." 2 Tim. 3:7

It's like being stuck in a revolving door fearful to get out and fearful that the floor will fall out from under our feet. As a child of God, the enemy of our souls will oppress us and try to hold us back from all God offers His children.

It requires an abiding "saint" (I mean that word in the truest sense), a believing believer, to let God point out blind spots. It isn't that I had never been a fearful person before; but the violent death of my parents had brought out and increased a tendency that was already within me.

For those of you reading this book who are experiencing demonic oppression I suggest you pray this prayer of personal repentance and intercession along with me. Right now, is the appointed day to begin the process and reckon the oppression the same as gone.

"Oh Lord, expose my pretended righteousness. Remove my idols – my coping mechanisms that are so much a part of my being that I don't know where they end, and I begin. Yes Lord, I take refuge in You. Help me to possess my heavenly inheritance and spiritual place." Amen

"I beseech You Lord; remove the <u>stumbling blocks</u> I have unknowingly placed before my sons and husband. Help them turn to You. I am sorrowful because of my sin. But I have faith that You have forgiven me, and I have joy that Your purpose for creating my family will not be frustrated. We do have willful hearts (intentions) and ways (actions). We need Your healing touch. You will lead us and reward us with Your comfort. May we be counted among the multitudes who love You and love to keep Your commandments." Hallelujah! Amen Isaiah 57:12-15,18-19 referenced in above prayer.

Isaiah 57:14-15,19b

"Build up, build up, prepare the way, remove every obstacle out of the way of My people."

"For thus says the high and exalted One Who lives forever. whose name is Holy, I dwell on a high and holy place, and also with the contrite and lowly of spirit. In order to revive the spirit of the lowly and to revive the heart of the contrite."

"Peace, peace to him who is far off (both Jew and Gentile) and to him that is near. Says the Lord, I will heal him." (explanation added)

As we seek God for the peace only He can give, our speech will sprout with thankful praise and healing will follow. (My paraphrase)

So, if sentimentalism is a dark road with a dead end where unfulfilled emotions go to die, then superstition is a step off the cliff.

C.S. Lewis said, "We wonder not that God has our best in mind. We wonder how painful His best will turn out to be."

That wondering can lead us to worship and praise. It can lead is us to agree with David when he said, "Thou hast enclosed me behind and before, and hast laid Thy hand upon me. Such knowledge is too wonderful for me." Ps. 139:5-6 KJV

(My paraphrase) – Such knowledge is too full of wonder for me to comprehend so I will not try to figure it out. I will just be grateful for it.

If that wondering doesn't lead us to praise, it can lead us to the underworld. The difference is spiritual life and death.

"If a wish is not translated into resolution
and then into <u>action</u>
it will translate itself into a corrupting
instead of a redeeming power in life."
Oswald Chambers <u>Still Higher for His Highest</u> February 18

What is this action that Oswald Chambers refers to?

It is obedience to the voice of God. He will take our desires and translate them into the blessed life.

There is a popular saying/question in some Christian circles. It is this, "What would Jesus do?"

Jesus, Himself, gave us the answer to that question.

He said, "I do nothing on My own initiative, but I speak these things as the Father taught Me. And He who sent Me is with Me; He has not left Me alone, for I always do the things that are pleasing to Him." John 8:28c-29

He was obedient to His Father's commands, and He performed many marvelous works. His public ministry and the actions of His personal life testified to His Divinity and His willingness to please the Father.

"Oh Lord, may our "actions" testify to Your indwelling Spirit's leading." Amen

Taking action in someone else's life is not the
same thing and may not be appropriate.

SUPERSTITION CAN BE A SUBTLE THING

Wanting something, even something good for someone else may be a sin. We may be trying to bring a wish into existence by the sheer force of our will. When our wishing and hoping dominates our minds it can be similar to trying to conjure it up. God forbid!

"Lord, not by will or by might but by Your Spirit." Zachariah 4:6

Just because something may seem like good intentions it may not be God's intentions.

So, what are we to do? Praying for discernment is always wise. Good is often the enemy of the best.

God might tell us to let the chips fall where they may. It's hard to do that when it seems like someone's life is falling apart. We may want to rush in and glue the pieces together in a pattern that pleases us. That seldom, if ever, works. But there are no rules or formulas. That's why learning to pray in the calm times prepares us for times of crisis. Those circumstances may cause us to experience a crisis of belief.

"Humble yourselves under the mighty hand of God. . .." 1 Peter 5:6

A modern rendering of that verse could be "calm yourself" under the mighty hand of God. He will allow us to fume, fuss, complain and rail against Him but He withholds His peace until we calm ourselves. He won't do it for us, but **He will do it through** us. Just don't forget that the hand of the Lord is mighty and ready to save when we are ready for Him to do His part.

Don't panic, take a deep breath and talk to yourself about who God is and how He has been faithful in the past. Recall specifics. Make a list of His past provisions if that helps. He is the same yesterday, today and forever. And be grateful that you are not alone.

Richard Foster said in his book <u>Life With God</u>, "A spiritual discipline is an **intentionally directed action**, which places us in a position to receive from God the power to do what we cannot accomplish on our own." (Emphasis mine)

C.S. Lewis said of God's dealings with us, "He seems to do nothing of Himself which He can possible delegate to His creatures. He commands us to do slowly and blunderingly what He could do perfectly and in the twinkling of an eye. Creation seems to be delegation through and through."

This is the kind of action that moves us down the road toward the Father who is waiting with open arms to receive a wayward child. (Luke 15:11-32)

PUTTING THE PIECES BACK TOGETHER IS GOD'S JOB

He wants a personal relationship with each one of His children. It's called practicing the presence for a reason. Practice makes perfect because perfect in this context means complete, wholehearted and mature. Yes, we and the ones we love will have growing pains, but it is worth all the trouble.

I love many kinds of art but one of my favorites is the mosaic. Tiny colorful chips placed lovingly in a pattern creates a thing of beauty. If you look closely at one small section, you do not see the big picture. God sees the whole picture of our lives and He knows best how to arrange all the pieces.

"Dear Father God, I thank you for invading my thoughts as I leaned over Clayton that night to give him one last hug, You honored my request for clarity concerning my true identity and my purpose in life. I acknowledged that I was a wife, a mother and a teacher, but I did not think of myself as a daughter. God the Father knew I needed to be reminded of my spiritual inheritance."

"Lord, You do the miraculous. We must do
our part. Show us what our part is.

Show us the intentionally directed action that places us in a position to receive power to do your will.

And give us peace that You are doing the part that only You can do.
You have heard our prayer. You are Jehovah
Jireh. You will see to it!" Amen

CHAPTER 3

LET GO AND LET GOD

Letting the chips fall where they may does not mean giving up.

In Romans 15:4 the apostle Paul tells us, "Whatever was written in earlier times was written for our instruction, that through perseverance and encouragement of the scriptures we might have hope."

Paul's prayer vs.5, 6 - "Now may the God who gives perseverance and encouragement grant you to be of the same mind with **one another** according to Christ Jesus."

Without Your wisdom Lord I struggle to know when I am being willful or when I am persevering. Please show me Lord. Encourage me as only You can.

Strong willed wishing	versus	**God willed perseverance**
Emotionally I get out of sorts and stressed because circumstances are the same or seem worse.		Emotionally I feel calm in spite of the lack of encouraging circumstances and I have HOPE.

"The peace of God passes all understanding." There is a calmness that makes no sense to the world because it is spiritually appropriated.

To appropriate means to accept, affirm, use, seize, utilize, and devote for a special purpose. Appropriating the Spirit of God is as easy as the simple prayer. Come Lord Jesus be my encouragement.

BEARING BURDENS – CARRYING YOUR OWN LOAD

Bear **one another's** burdens and thus fulfill the law of Christ. Gal. 6:2

Each one shall bear his own load. Gal. 6:5

For where two or three have gathered together in My name there I am in their midst. Matt. 18:20

If we try to carry the load of another person, those issues God has assigned to them as a means of fellowship with Himself, we will get sidetracked. God's grace is available to them for their own individual needs. When my parents died, I knew my brother would go to God for himself. Each of us had our own load, but we certainly did help each other bear up under the burden of loss and pain.

The "one another" term implies a give and take where two or more people are answerable to God as they share their lives. When we come together each one has some things to give away and some things to take away from the encounter. It implies unity among believers. (1 Corinthians 14:15 referenced)

Jesus's prayer – "That they may all be one even as Thou, Father, art in Me, and I in Thee, that they may be in Us". John 17:21

Compassion and empathy are from the Lord. Sentimentality or sympathy taken too far imply, "You should not have to suffer like this. Surely, you shall not die, I will shelter you."

That kind of sympathy takes the nerve away from the one being sympathized with.

We are strong in the Lord when we are united in the common goal of dying to self, resisting the devil and walking with God.

From the start of His plan for mankind He pronounced the everlasting truth about His kind intentions toward His loved ones.

Ex. 19:6a God said to the people, "You shall be to Me a kingdom of priests and a holy nation."

This covenant spoken of by God was for Israel's being God's own possession – His treasure. In this kingdom all the citizens were priests with direct access to Him.

Ex. 20: 18 "And all the people perceived the thunder and the lightning flashes and the sound of the trumpet and the mountain smoking; and when the people saw it, they said to Moses, speak to us yourself and we will listen; but let not God speak to us, lest we die." In their stubborn self-will they sympathized with each other.

The Israelites wanted Moses to go up on the mountain, get a word from God and then carry their load for them. Because they had a "go between person" they could choose to say NO to him. After all Moses was not God. He was a man like themselves. We all can see what a disaster that was. As soon as he was out of sight their lack of personal relationship with God became evident. They created an idol with their own hands and worshiped it instead of God.

Father, You said, "Come now, and let us reason together, though your sins are as scarlet they will be as white as snow." Is. 1:18

The Spirit says, "Come." How can we deny the Lord the desire of His heart? He paid a huge price to make a way for us to fellowship with Himself. He must love us very much.

Words of an old hymn-
Trust Me – Try Me
Prove Me saith the Lord of Hosts
And see if a blessing
Unmeasured blessing
I will not pour out on thee.

Take a chance. Risk not getting your own way. Trust Him enough to speak to Him about the burdens you have been trying to carry all by yourself. Try listening to Him and He will **prove** Himself to be more **wonderful** than you ever imagined.

For further study read: Exodus 19 The giving of the Law and the Covenant accepted

Exodus 20 The Ten Commandments

OUR TRUE PURPOSE

We humans have age old questions.

Where did we come from? Why are we here? What is our purpose?

Perhaps we should be asking what was God's
purpose for creating mankind?

Some would say our purpose as Christians is to proclaim the saving grace
of Jesus Christ. That certainly would be true. But there is a deeper purpose.

David Wilkerson put it this way:

"The Father's will from creation – His entire purpose behind the birth
of mankind – was to create a body of fellowship for His Son. From the very
beginning, we see the Lord seeking communion with man. His Spirit walked
with Adam in the Garden of Eden, conversing in the cool of the day."

"And then there was Enoch who "walked with God and he was not, for
God took him." (Gen. 5:24) Enoch was a young man of 365 years. Most
people lived twice that long back then. It is as though our Lord hungered
for Enoch's company so much that He brought him on to heaven so that
they could walk in uninterrupted communion. It is our inheritance to
satisfy that God ordained hunger." (close quote)

We don't think of the omnipotent God as being hungry for anything
and especially not hungry for anything we have to offer. But we are created

in His image so it should not surprise us so much that our hunger for God originates in His hunger to commune with us.

Someone once said," I am His pleasure when He is my treasure."

To feed Christ we must rest in His presence and anticipate His words will come and speak life to us.

The woman at the well in John 4:5-42 is an illustration of how important it is to respond to Christ's call for fellowship.

Jesus was going about His Father's business. He invited her to enter into conversation and she accepted the invitation.

> She brought to Him an honest seeking heart
> and as He spoke, she listened closely.
> She heeded His words spoken to her.
> She served Him water, believed Him and took action.

Their interaction fulfilled Christ's need for fellowship. It was a communion that was satisfying to Jesus.

Notice, He spoke to her first. Speaking to a Samaritan woman was not customary. The Samaritans were hated by the Jews because of their mixed Jewish and Gentile blood. But He did it anyway. Our God delights in breaking with man's traditions when they are a hinderance to fellowship. He said to her, "Give Me a drink."

What happened next was a dialogue. It was not the prescribed words of a theatrical play. It was the miracle of true dialogue that can bring relationship into being. The one necessity is that both must enter in and really listen to each other. As the dialogue proceeded, she asks a question. Jesus answers using the words "living water." She is intrigued and she wants to hear more. The dialogue continues. Jesus tells her things about herself that prove He is at the very least a prophet.

He said to her, "Go call your husband, and come here," The woman answered and said, 'I have no husband'; Jesus said to her, "You have well said, I have no husband for you have had five husbands, and the one whom you now have is not your husband." Verses 16-17

She questioned further and when the moment was right, Jesus revealed His true identity to her.

The woman said to Him, "I know that Messiah is coming (He who is called Christ)." Jesus said to her, "I who speak to you am He."

We know the Samaritan women believed that He was the Messiah because she, in turn, witnessed to others who also believed. She said," Come see a man, which told me all things that I ever did. Is this not the Christ?"

While Jesus and the woman were conversing, the disciples went to the city to purchase food. When they returned they said, "Rabbi, eat." But He said to them, "I have food to eat that you do not know about. My food is to do the will of Him who sent Me, and to accomplish His work." Verses 31-34

Jesus proceeded to teach them about the fields of lost souls that are white and ready for harvest. Kingdom work is witnessing of the saving grace of our Lord's death and resurrection.

We minister to Him by listening patiently. We are not doing God a favor by listening. Listening is the very least we can do for One who has done so much for us. After all, when we listen with an honest heart we benefit greatly.

The Samaritan woman is an example of a women whose behavior up till now was not an example of virtue. Jesus knew that. He could have destroyed her with harsh condemnation. But instead He spoke of truth and He spoke the truth with love. She did not need to go home and clean up her life before the blessed dialogue could continue. Jesus' confrontation was gentle but direct. He did not condemn her, nor did He excuse her behavior.

He just loved her.

C.S. Lewis prayed this prayer for the lost.

"Lord keep on loving them till You love them into loving You."

Pause and think about the love of God that constrains us. He persuades us and urges us to love Him. He holds us lovingly in arms that could destroy us with a flick of His mighty finger. Instead, with the hand that was pierced for us He touches the sin that so easily entangles us. His power untangles and sets us free to flourish as He intended and to accomplish our God given purpose of fellowship with the Son.

Praise God!

Selah – Pause and think on these things.

CHAPTER 5

TWO MORE HONEST SEEKING HEARTS

Two Men on the Road to Emmaus

The desire of God's heart is to walk with us and talk with us and tell us we are His own. . . . so that we learn to recognize Him.

In Luke 24: 13-35 God gives us another example of honest seeking hearts. The two disciples on the road from Jerusalem to Emmaus give us insight into our Lords desire to commune with His loved ones.

Our God is the God who ordered by command the world to be called into existence. Not only does He order by command, but He does things in an order that we would do well to pay attention to.

After the crucifixion, burial and His glorious resurrection, the first thing He did was appear to two men walking on the road to Emmaus. They were devastated to hear of Christ's death.

"While they were conversing and discussing, Jesus Himself, approached and began traveling with them. But their eyes were prevented from recognizing Him." Luke 24:15-16

They didn't understand that the Old Testament prophecies were being fulfilled concerning Jesus. If they had known the scriptures they would have known He had to die and be resurrected. (Luke 24:27) . He told them all about it. But before He explained the prophecies of His coming, the significance of His death, burial and resurrection, He did something remarkable. The first thing He did was exactly what He had done with the woman at the well. He asked them a question that began a give and take conversation. He said, "What are you talking about?"

Why did He choose to walk and talk with these two men? I believe He knew they were honestly seeking to know truth and would listen to Him, feeding His need for fellowship. The three of them did enjoy sweet fellowship. When Jesus said it was time for Him to move on "They said, stay with us, for it is getting toward evening, and the day is now nearly over. And He went in to stay with them." (Vs. 29) They still did not know He was their Lord, but their hearts burned within them while He was explaining the scriptures to them. (vs. 32)

I will speak for myself when I say that I didn't seek a close relationship with my Lord for years after my new birth. I went through the motions and followed some rules, but my heart was not burning within me. It was lukewarm at best. But I am very grateful that before my parent's death I did begin to recognize His voice and rejoice in His presence.

These two gave Jesus the response He wanted. He went in to tarry with them. (24:29) They had fed Christ's need for communion and now He took them to His table where He fed them. "It came about that when He reclined at the table with them, He took bread and blessed it, and breaking it, He began giving it to them. And their eyes opened, and they recognized Him; and He vanished from their sight." (24:31)

Instead of going on to Emmaus they returned to Jerusalem where the eleven disciples and those who were with them had gathered together.

Because the two were not satisfied with an initial encounter and asked Him to stay longer. They had the testimony of a lifetime. "The Lord appeared to us! We talked with Him and ate with Him. I tell you we saw him alive. And He fed us God's Word from His own mouth. Yes, He is alive and well." (Paraphrase vs. 33-35)

I believe Jesus wanted their fellowship. He wanted to calm their fears, encourage their hearts and He wanted this incident recorded for our benefit. Today He wants to calm our fears and encourage us as we go deeper into relationship with Him. He wants to walk with us up and down this road we are on. Whether we are going through the shadow of death or walking down the aisle to be married and then out the door to begin a new phase of life.

Someday in heaven I want to meet these two men and thank them for their single-minded devotion. When we are double minded we are unstable. God lets us experience instability and discontent until all our fresh springs are in Him. "Like a roadway in the wilderness, rivers in the desert." (Is. 43:19). He is ever ready to give us Living Water.

Oswald Chambers put it this way in his devotion for Oct. 12, <u>My Utmost for His Highest</u>;

"The worth of a man is revealed in his attitude to ordinary things when he is not before the footlights."

The following is an excerpt from my prayer journal.

DEEPER AND LOWER

In the past, I thought the Christian life was one of progressing onward and upward. That would mean that I would become better behaved. This of course would be noticeable to everyone and possibly resulting in a "named" position in the church.

NONE OF THIS IS TRUE!

God's proper perspective for me is one of going deeper in personal relationship with Him and a realization that the smaller I become the bigger He becomes in my awareness.

What have I got to lose?

Only my pride that puts me in opposition to The-God-Of-The-Universe.

"Dear Lord, today I choose to go lower!

Lord give me deeper gratitude for all You have
done, are doing and will do for me.

Lord, give me deeper repentance.

Lord, give me deeper trust.

Give me deeper knowledge of You my Savior, Master and Lord.

Give me deeper power in private prayer.

Give me deeper holiness while remembering that I
am nothing unless you make something of me. I have
nothing unless Your grace gives it to me. Amen

Martin Luther quote-

"God created the world out of nothing. If we remember
that we are nothing then God can make something out
of us."

By contrast we are worthless when we are compared to God. But, by
the breath of His mouth, the "dust" we are made of becomes the clay He
uses to mold us into His image.

"Then the Lord God formed man of dust from the ground and
breathed into his nostrils the breath of life; and became a living being."
Genesis 2:7

The deeper lessons of faith are to be highly valued.

On the evening of February 20, after writing these words, I opened the
book Jesus Calling to see the Deeper and Lower theme repeated. Someone
once said that when you pray coincidences happen, blessed miraculous
"coincidences."

"Learn to live from your true Center in Me. I reside in
the deepest depths of your being, in eternal union with

your spirit. It is at this deep level that My Peace reigns continually. You will not find lasting peace in the world around you, in circumstances, or in human relationships. The external world is always in flux under the curse of death and decay. But there is a gold mine of Peace deep within you, waiting to be tapped. Take time to delve into the riches of My residing Presence. I want you to live increasingly from your real Center, where My Love has an eternal grip on you. I am Christ in you, the hope of Glory."

Sarah Young

THANK YOU, PRECIOUS HOLY SPIRIT.

CHAPTER 6

THE STORY OF THE TWO DAUGHTERS

I do not doubt the historical accuracy of this story, but I believe it is also an allegory. As such it must not contradict any other truth in the Bible. It must add more depth and clarify the truth.

Mark 5:21-43

Beginning of the Story

Jairus, the synagogue official, came to Jesus and said, "My little daughter is at the point of death. Please come that You may lay your hands on her, that she may get well and live."

Jesus started walking with him to see the girl.

Middle of the Story

There was a woman who had a hemorrhage for 12 years. She had spent all her money and gone to many physicians who had not helped her. She had actually gotten worse. She was spiritually and financially bankrupt, but everything was about to change.

While many were crowding around Jesus; she said, "If I just touch His garments, I will get well."

"She reached out to Him. And Jesus immediately perceived in Himself that the power proceeding from him had gone forth."

Jesus asked, "Who touched Me?" She reluctantly answered that she had done this. Jesus said something very significant to her. He said, "Daughter, your faith has made you well, go in peace."

End of the Story

Someone came and said to Jairus, "Your daughter is dead do not bother the teacher anymore."

Jesus spoke words that should make any parent in this situation rejoice. He said," Do not be afraid any longer, only believe."

He said that she was not dead; only sleeping.

Jesus went to the girl, took her hand and said, "Little girl, I say to you, arise!"

She got up and began to walk. To the adults in the room; He said, "Feed her."

Now for the allegory:

The Young Daughter

He did not say, "Arise your sins are forgiven" or "Your faith has made you well." He did not call her, "Daughter." She was Jairus' daughter. A daughter after the flesh. She had interestingly been alive for the same amount of time that the woman had been bleeding. I am not sure of the full significance of that except that the number twelve symbolizes the power of God, His authority and the completion of a thing. And, it does seem to be evidence of a link between the two daughters.

I think the younger daughter represents the unbeliever whatever their actual age. The ones who are skeptical about God. Those whose eyes are closed in the rictus of spiritual death. Now she has had an encounter with the Savior. She had a Red Sea experience. Now she can choose whether to walk out her new life in faith or reject Him as her Savior. It is the responsibility of the older generation to feed her the pure food of the Word.

- The Older Daughter -

She had been bleeding from a place of intimacy. Life is in the blood and hers had been flowing from her for a very long time. The lifelessness of many churches today reveals the same problem. They are all about Jesus like the crowd of people. I can identify with them. For years I was "all about Jesus" bumping into Him on occasion. He actually did bring healing times to me, but I did not realize that all those verses about seeking, knocking and asking were meant for me to grow in relationship with my Father, embrace my daughterhood and my birthright.

Here lies the promise of the ages.

It is our inheritance as believers to live an exchanged life full of the resurrection life of our Savior.

That power is revealed in a loosening of the powers of heaven in the lives of those who come after us and in binding of the powers of darkness that would try to destroy us all.

It has been said that the Old Testament contains the new and the New Testament explains the old.

MOSES – GOD'S MAN OF THE HOUR

So, let us look at how our God interacted with the experienced generation and the less experienced generation of Moses' time.

Moses speaks to the older generation. He reminds them to love the Lord their God and always keep His charges, His statutes, His ordinances and His commands. Deut. 11:1

There are lists of specific actions that the Lord commands them to do but it is really their heart He is after. "You shall love the Lord your God with all your heart and with all your soul and with all your might . . . and you shall teach (these things) diligently to your sons." Deut. 5:5, 7. "Oh that they had such a heart in them, that they would fear Me and keep all My commandments always, that it may be well with them and with their sons forever!" Deut. 5:29

Moses goes on to recount miracles God did in Egypt, their Red Sea deliverance when Pharaoh's army was destroyed and their wilderness experience. In effect, Moses says, "You have no excuse to live in rebellion. You have seen His mighty hand and His outstretched arm of protection." My paraphrase Deut. 11:7

The older of the two daughters in Mark chapter five represents those of us who have reason to have our faith exercised. The same ones that God spoke to in Deut. 11:2 when He said, "I am not talking to your sons, who have not known and who have not seen the discipline of the Lord our God – His greatness, His mighty hand and His outstretched arm." (His arm of protection.) I am talking to you because, "Your own eyes have seen the great work of the Lord which He did." Deut. 11:7

We must reach out and break through the tiles of our own fear and unbelief. Our precious loved ones will wake up exactly when God reaches out to them, touches their hand, wakes them from the stupor they are in and speaks life to them. He knows all the details that have to come together before the time is right.

God spoke to the experienced generation, in Deut. 11:19 . He reminded them to teach their sons, talking of the commands when they sit in their house and when they walk along the road and when theylie down and when they rise up." Then He said that He was setting before them two choices, "I am setting before you today a blessing and a curse; the blessing if you listen to the commandments of the Lord your God, which I am commanding you today; and a curse, if you do not listen to the commandments of the Lord your God, but turn aside from the way which I am commanding you today, by following other gods (idols) which you have not known." Deut. 11:26-28 (Emphasis mine)

Everyone needed an encounter with the Sovereign Lord. They needed more than an intellectual assent. They needed a breathtaking realization that sin was crouching at the door and nothing short of surrender to the Lord God Jehovah would wipe their slate clean.

> Jesus has dealt with the curse . . . "Everyone who
> hangs on the tree is cursed." Galatians. 3:13
> The Father's plan is to reverse the curse of sin
> through Jesus dying on the cross in our place.
> He will set us apart (sanctify us), show us the way,
> and never leave or forsake us.

We are part of God's divine providence. We are an intricate part of this process called life in God.

That process is full of uncertainties and challenges that press us into loving our God. We aren't really aware of the true desire of our heart. It is through the stresses and the strains of life with God that we wake up to our individual callings and it takes many changes of the heart to come to places of peace. The give and take required can seem more like a wrestling match than a walk in the park.

Let each of us ask God a question.

Lord, what are You commanding me to do today?
I hear You say, "Love and obey."

Love and obey! Obey how? What action shall I perform?
What idols do I need to denounce in my life?

Deut. 13:4 Listen to The Voice. The Voice says . . .

"You shall **follow** the Lord your God and **fear** Him; and shall **keep His commandments, <u>listen to His voice</u>, serve** Him and <u>**cling to Him**</u>." Deut. 13:4 (emphasis added)

"Love the Lord your God, to WALK in all His ways and **<u>hold fast to Him</u>**." Deut. 11:22 (Emphasis added)

With the Voice comes the strength to hold on to Him for the "dear life" He has planned for us.

JACOB'S SPECIAL ENCOUNTER WITH GOD

Jacob, in the book of Genesis chapter 32 illustrates someone who has known God personally. He has listened to God. They have had dialogue together. He is returning to his father's land as a prince rich in flocks, herds, and servants. By worldly standards of the day he was a smashing success. God had kept His promise to bring him back to the land of his father safely while providing for all his needs.

The night before he was to come face to face with Esau his brother, who blamed him for the loss of his inheritance, Jacob had a very special encounter with God. Jacob was all alone having sent wives and children across the river with all his possessions. We are told that, "A man wrestled with him until daybreak." In the <u>darkness</u>, God allowed Himself to be overcome by Jacob but in the tussle Jacob's hip joint was dislocated. "God said, let Me go for dawn is breaking." But, like the two on the road to Emmaus, Jacob did not settle for that. Jacob said, "I will not let You go until You bless me." He clung to the man and held fast to Him. God blessed his persistence and changed his name from Jacob to Israel which means "he fights or persists with God" in prevailing prayer.

Words of the chorus:

I Will Change Your Name

I will change your name, you shall no longer be called
Wounded, Outcast, Lonely or Afraid.

I will change your name, your new name shall be
Confident, Joyfulness, Over-coming one,
Faithfulness, Friend of God, One who seeks My face.

Author Unknown

Dan Allender, commentary on Matthew –

"Those who trust God most are those whose faith permits them to risk wrestling with Him over the deeper issues of life. Good hearts are captured in a divine wrestling match; <u>fearful</u> hearts stay clear of the mat. The commitment to wrestle will be honored by God Who will not only break, but bless."

There's that word fearful; the kind of fear that is a symptom of the illness of unbelief. The woman with the issue of blood had to exhaust every other avenue before she reached out to her Savior. But she did reach out. She did it and so can we.

Correctly placed fear is the awe and admiration that inspires us to show up and walk on listening to the Lord's voice. That blessed kind of fear inspires us to serve Him the food of fellowship. As we cling to Him and, "Hold fast to the Word of Life." Philippians 2:16 (my paraphrase)

Praise You Lord, Your mercies are new every morning. Please, bless us with an honest seeking heart that cries out, "I will not let You go until You bless me even if it cost me something I hold dear.

Amen

> "To pray is to change. This is a great grace. How good of God to provide a path whereby our lives can be taken over by love and joy and peace and patience and kindness and goodness and faithfulness and gentleness and self-control."
>
> Richard J. Foster

Another excerpt from my prayer journal:

REVIVE US OH LORD

I love the Bible verse, "Revive me, Oh Lord, according to Thy word." Psalm 119:107 ." As I ponder those words and remember the prophecies about revival in the last days before our Lord's return, I think in terms of the tide of sin being turned back. I hope for a return to days when our Lord was honored in our land. Without realizing it I expect people to fill church buildings, for crusades to flourish or that something noticeable will happen. It would be wonderful if those things did happen, but we must not wait to see outward signs. Instead, let us look to ourselves. Have we chosen this day whom we will serve? Matthew 4:10a

My prayer –

> "Please Lord, come work behind the scenes as You please.
> Send dreams and visions of Your glory.
> Awaken in our hearts a renewed desire to share the gospel one on one
> and in new and different ways.
> Lord, guard our hearts and minds from thinking we
> will display our talents in the days to come.
> The smallest action at your bidding has eternal
> significance.(Matt.25:40 paraphrase)
> Help us really believe that is true!

Psalms 98:1 "Oh sing to the Lord a new song. For He has done wonderful things."

Isaiah 43:18-19 "Do not call to mind the former things or ponder things of the past. Behold I will do something new. Now it will spring forth; will you not be aware of it? I will even make a roadway in the wilderness, rivers in the desert."

Lord, why should we expect it to look like it has looked before?

Call it revival or call it by another name You are quite able to evangelize anyone who comes to You in simple faith. You, Lord God Almighty, will prepare Your bride, heal the spiritually sick and give eternal life to the dying who have an advocate crying out to You on their behalf. Matt.9:18 paraphrased

So, I pray . . . "Come Lord Jesus. Pour out Your Spirit any way You choose. Use those of us who have exhausted all our human resources and have come to the end of ourselves. Give us courage to reach out and touch the hem of your garment. We have bled from a place of intimacy long enough." Mark 5:25-29

"Please Lord, reach out and touch those You know are spiritually dead but are not without hope. Come Lord, reach out and touch them so they wake to the reality of Your calling in their lives. Let it be according to Your word. Please create a hunger for Yourself, and while You are at it, prepare us to feed the newly awakened life in them." Matt.5:41-43

Will we be aware of it? "Lord make us aware and show us the way to that road in the wilderness. Cause our hearts to burn within us as we perceive with ever increasing clarity the workings of Your kingdom here on earth." Is. 43:19 , Luke 24:32 , Matt. 6:10

"When the moment is right, when Your bride is ready **please** come and snatch us away to be with You forever." Amen

Written on October 15th, 2015

My Cherished Dream of Glory

On September 23rd I slept through the alarm because I was dreaming. The dream was delightful.

I saw no scenery, just an unavoidable open space in front of me and an unavoidable presence there. The space was the brightest whiteness I have ever seen. It was pure and clean.

My very first emotion was that of puzzlement. I wasn't sure who the Being was. I wondered if this could be some silly schoolgirl crush. I had never had a dream like this but the moment I realized that my beloved husband was standing nearby I knew the Being was Jesus. The emotion I felt at that moment was of a very happy person deeply in love, longing to embrace the Being. I was flooded with love. The word cherish comes to mind. I felt reverence, esteem, adoration and surprising calmness all at the same time. I was loved by Him and I loved Him in return. I cannot over emphasize the rapture I experienced in those few moments. In the days following my dream the two words that seemed to dominate my mind concerning the dream were cherish and rapture.

Rapture defined is an expression or manifestation of ecstasy or passion; a state of being carried away with overwhelming emotion and a mystical experience in which the spirit is exalted to a knowledge of divine things.

That dictionary definition is perfect and describes my experience very well. I can only imagine that at the last trump, "Those who are dead and those who are alive and remain will be caught up to be with the Lord" and experience the rapture of joy inexpressible and full of glory. The precious moments of my dream are but a foretaste of the joy to come.

> Thank you, Lord Jesus for making the way for we sinful humans to come boldly into your presence. Thank you for the privilege of very special moments like my dream and for every moment we have as we experience your presence. Come, Lord Jesus!

As God would have it later the same day as my dream, a customer of our HVAC business gave Mike a book. That book was about a women's dream of heaven. I am convinced that God used this book to confirm that my dream was in fact of Jesus. And I believe that the dream was an answer to my prayer that God send dreams and visions to whomever He chooses and whenever He chooses.

Dearest Lord, I am willing to be a receiver of dreams and visions. Please be a shield about me. I covet Your protection so that the enemy does not steal my vitality and energy and that dreams are from You . . . visions while awake are from You and You only. I am not seeking in the sense of longing for an experience apart from You, Lord. Please help me preserve the memory of this cherished dream of glory.

Amen

CHAPTER 7

RELAX – RELATE – RELY – RELINQUISH CONTROL

Years ago, I found myself at the chiropractor's office. I had never gone to a chiropractor before, but I was suffering ironically from a stiff neck. The Bible describes being "stiff necked" as spiritually stubborn. Our God does have a sense of humor. When the painful process was over, I began to see the humor in it. But during the process there was nothing to laugh about. Dr. Bebermyer was a Christian man with a wonderful reputation but I found myself in an unfamiliar situation and the process was physically painful. Each time I went I slowly began to heal. But he always had to remind me to relax. One day he said something that changed my life. He said, "We can do this the easy way, or we can do this the hard way. It's not harder for me. You're making it harder on yourself." I realized in that moment that I was resisting the process and when I relaxed the pain of each treatment was actually lessened. Also, I progressed more quickly through the treatment because I relinquished control and let him have it. After all, I made the appointment, showed up at his office and paid for his service, so why did I resist his capable hands? Because I was double minded. I wanted his help, but I wanted it to be painless and easy. I had not learned to see God in everything around me. Nor had I learned how to enter into His sufferings. You see when we hurt, He hurts also. At first, I did not relate to the doctor as a person sent by God to facilitate the healing of my body and teach me a valuable lesson. I instinctively knew he cared about his patients and after his kindly rebuke I was able to relax and rely on him to have my best interest in mind. The process did require something of me. I had to show up, submit, accept that some pain was required for healing, exercise faith and express my gratitude to the doctor and the God who orchestrated the whole experience.

We have a saying at my church, "God will be as gentle as He can be to achieve His purpose in our lives."

I am reminded of the words of an old hymn:

"Oh, what peace we often forfeit, oh what needless pain we bear,
　　All because we will not carry everything to Him in prayer."

Michael Wells put it this way, "God permits and prevents only those things that will bring about our finishing well."

The Dr. Bebermyer experience went far beyond relieving my stiff neck pain. The process set in motion one of many spiritual healings. Just like the symphony conductor directs the orchestra, our God orchestrates our lives if we let Him. Each one of us has an instrument to play. Just like the body has many parts but just one head. Dr. Bebermyer showed a frightened young mother that sometimes physical pain is a symptom of spiritual illness or at the very least physical pain tests us. It tests those of us who have no excuse to live in rebellion. We have seen the outstretched arm of protection.

We really can give thanks in all things, even those
things we do not like or understand because He causes
all things to work together for our good.
Eph. 5:20, Rom. 8:28

James 1:3 "The testing of our faith produces endurance." And it produces single-minded devotion to the Lord.

There is more to the story. I went to the good doctor in the spring of that year and by fall my overall health was improved and I was well enough to homeschool our two sons. When we relax, rely and relinquish control there are blessings tucked inside blessings, tucked inside sorrows and pain.

Some day in heaven God will more than make up to us for all our pain and loss.

Why does He allow such great suffering? Only God really knows the answer to that question in every detail, but we do know that creation groans under the penalty of sin and death.

Jesus wept at the tomb of Lazarus. We are not told why He wept. Possibly it was because of the sin that leads to sickness and death. He certainly wasn't weeping for Lazarus because he knew that for the sake of his loved ones and for the sake of students of the Bible, Lazarus would come back to life. I wonder if Lazarus was glad to be back or sorry to leave paradise.

In relating to people these days, we often toss around the phrase, "Would you do me a favor?" It's usually something trivial. But the word "grace" means favor. Jesus did us a great favor when He took the penalty for our sin. It is a grace greater than all our sins.

Praise You, Jesus, our Redeemer. Yours is the Name above all names. We bow before You in awe of Your greatness and kindness toward us. Show us the part we are to play and lead us into harmony with You. Amen

GOD IS AT WORK IN THIS WORLD TO WILL HIS GOOD PLEASURE. HE WILL INVITE US TO ENTER IN.

The following is an excerpt from George Muller's autobiography:

George Muller's life is an example to us all. In his autobiography he describes for us the way he learned to listen to God, hold fast to Him and enter into ministry.

George was born in 1805 and died in 1898 at the age of ninety three. He was known as a man of great faith. He established orphanages in England, and he depended on God for all his needs. In 1841, at the age of 36, he discovered something that changed his life.

He said, "I saw more clearly than ever, that the first great and primary business to which I ought to attend every day was, to have my soul happy in the Lord. The first thing to be concerned about was not, how much I might serve the Lord, how I might glorify the Lord; but how I might get my soul into a happy state, and how my inner man might be nourished."

He went on to explain in more detail the practice of meditation.

"The first thing I did, after having asked a few words of the Lord's blessing upon His precious Word, was to begin to meditate on the Word of God; searching, as it were, into every verse, to get a blessing out of it; not for the sake of the public ministry of the Word; not for the sake of preaching on what I had meditated upon; but for the sake of obtaining food for my own soul. The result I have found to be almost invariably this, that after a very few minutes my soul has been led to confession, or to thanksgiving, or to supplication, so that though I did not, as it were, give myself to prayer, but to meditation, yet it turned almost immediately more or less into prayer.

No public ministry ever brought the matter before me. No private intercourse with a brother stirred me up to this matter. And yet now, since God has taught me this point, it is as plain to me as anything that the first thing the child of God has to do morning by morning is to obtain food for his inner man.

Now what is the food for the inner man: not prayer, but the Word of God; and here again not the simple reading of the Word of God, so that it only passes through our minds, just as water runs through a pipe, but considering what we read, pondering over it, and applying it to our hearts . . . "Autobiography of George Muller comp. Fred Bergen (London: j.Nisvet.1906.) 152-4 (end of quote)

George Muller's Holy Spirit directed goal was to get himself into a happy state of mind and let the word of God nourish his inner man. The people around him were blessed and I am convinced that the Lord enjoyed every minute of their time together.

If we apply ourselves to the scriptures the way George Mueller did the Holy Spirit will meet us there and it will become a necessary blessing.

The Work of the Holy Spirit in this Age

The work of the Holy Spirit, in this age we live in, is to convict the world of sin. Our conscience alone will not do the job. It cannot be trusted because our conscience often comes up with excuses for our sin.

Jesus said, "And He (The Holy Spirit) when He comes will convict the world concerning sin . . . because they do not believe in Me."

He is to convince/persuade the world of Jesus' complete and utter righteousness. No amount of head knowledge can do this and no work on our part is needed.

As He convicts and convinces those who are open to His call, the body of believers is formed for fellowship with the Son.

Jesus said, "I go - He comes."

Since Jesus is not here in bodily form the Holy Spirit speaks for Him.

"When the Helper comes, whom I will send to you from the Father, that is the Spirit of truth, who proceeds from the Father, He will bear witness of Me." John 15:26

It takes a supernatural act of the Spirit to convert and restore us to fellowship with this triune God, the Three in One, and cleans us from all our sin.

Jesus also said, "Truly I say to you unless you are converted and become like children, you shall not enter the kingdom of heaven." Matthew 18:3

We are exceedingly blessed by the Holy Spirit's ministry of indwelling each of us. He comes to abide and reside in this mortal body and help us remain constantly aware of His presence in our lives.

Paul said, "Do you not know that your body is a temple of the Holy Spirit?" 1 Corinthians 6:19

In John 15:9 Jesus said, "Just as the Father has loved Me, I have also loved you: abide (remain) in My love." Also, in John 14:26 He said, "But the Helper, the Holy Spirit, whom the Father will send in My name, He will teach you all things, and bring to your remembrance all that I said to you." John 14:26

He will speak for Jesus, teach us and remind us of the truth that the law does not save us.

Galatians 2:20-21 Paul said, ". . . Christ lives in me; and the life which I now live in the flesh I live by faith in the Son of God, who loved me, and delivered Himself up for me; (in my place). I do not nullify the grace of God; for if righteousness comes through the law, then Christ died needlessly."

It is Holy Spirit's job to lead us in God's ways down His chosen path for each of us. It is there that we are free to bear spiritual fruit that is eternal. No fake fruit made by human hands, but supernatural fruit that is food for the lost world or for our brothers and sisters in Christ.

***** The root determines the fruit. *****

John 15:5 "I am the vine, you are the branches; he who abides in Me and I in him, he bears much fruit; for apart from Me you can do nothing."

The Holy Spirit will produce in us a desire to see other people accept Jesus' invitation for salvation. It will be a natural progression to bear witness to Jesus' saving grace.

He gives us HOPE. Our faith is founded in hope of the past work of Christ and our hope is grounded in the future promises of Christ. The Holy Spirit's work in this age is to make His truth a reality to us.

When we are weak and don't know what to pray, He intercedes for us.

Romans 8:26-28
"The Spirit also helps our weakness; for we do not know how to pray as we should, but the Spirit Himself intercedes for us with groaning too deep for words; and He who searches the hearts knows what the mind of the Spirit is, because He intercedes for the saints according to the will of God. And we know that God causes all things to work together for good to those who love God, to those who are called according to His purpose."

Praise God we are never alone in our sin, our sorrow or our joy. Jesus said, "He would never desert us or ever forsake us." (fail, leave or reject us.) Hebrews 13:5 (My paraphrase)

To top it all off He empowers us to live the life He has chosen for us. We don't just barely get by. We can live life to the fullest and rise to every occasion God allows to come our way.

Zechariah 4:6 "Not by might nor by power, but by My Spirit, says the Lord of Hosts."

What a blessed relief to know that the triune God; the Father, Son and Holy Spirit have not abandoned us to our own finite resources, but Their loving kindnesses are like the stars of the universe.

God's names in the original language of the Bible reveal much about His character.

He is Elohim, the <u>Creator</u> of all things and the <u>Sustainer</u> of all things. Elohim created us with the capacity to love, honor and worship Him. The less empty of self we are, the less blessing God can pour into us. The more we are self-sufficient and proud the less eternal fruit we can bear. How wonderful of Him to arrange things so that we are shown when we are "full of ourselves."

He is El-Shaddai, the One who fills us and makes us fruitful says; "Without Me ye can do nothing." John 15:5

As believers in Jesus Christ our sin is completely covered. We are justified before the Father. It is just-as-if-we-had-never-sinned. But the process of nourishing the Spirit in us and starving the "old man nature" requires Holy Spirit intervention. He is the One who fills us and makes us fruitful.

"Greater love has no one than this, that one lay down his life for his friends." John 15:13

Thank You Jesus for willingly laying down Your life for us and sending Your Spirit to indwell and empower us to willingly spend our lives for others. Thank You Holy Spirit for gently and persistently clearing away hindrances to our worship, getting our souls nourished and in a happy state in the Lord. Amen

Lamentations 3:19-23

The prophet Jeremiah laments, that is, he cries aloud to the Lord. He says:

"Remember my affliction and my wandering,
the wormwood and bitterness.
Surely my soul remembers and is bowed down within me.

This I recall to my mind; therefore, I have hope.
The Lord's loving kindnesses indeed never cease,
for His compassions never fail. They are new
every morning; great is His faithfulness."

PRAISE GOD, HIS FAITHFULLNESS IS
UNPARRALELED AND THERE IS NO END!

CHAPTER 8

MY "TESTIMONY" IN A COURT OF LAW

The two men on the road to Emmaus testified to an encounter with Jesus Christ when they recounted their experience to other people. They were distressed because of the situation they found themselves in. They did not understand that Jesus had a plan which could only be fulfilled by His dying and coming back to life. The encounter was not sought after. It was not their idea. They could have been too stressed out to speak to a stranger, but they rose to the occasion. They spoke the truth to other people when given the opportunity, and they were blessed in the process. They gave God what they had, and He worked with it to accomplish His will. (Luke 24:13-35 referenced)

I mention this Bible story because there are parallels to it and the story from my own life that I am about to tell you.

I need to take you back to 2018 and explain the events that led up to my experience in the court room. It was an incredibly stressful year. My husband and I had closed our HVAC business. To add to that we had gotten the news that our family from Iowa could not come for Thanksgiving holiday. It would probably be another whole year before we saw them. The other news I received was a summons to jury duty. I was immediately gripped with the fear that I would be called to be a juror on a murder trial. Even though it had been 38 years since my parent's death painful memories flooded back to my mind.

On September 10th I arrived at the courthouse in downtown Tulsa. The first day was uneventful. I met some nice people to visit with and we passed the time away. It was not until the next day that my name was called to be on a jury.

Forty-five people were escorted to a large hall just outside the courtroom. We sat there and waited to be called inside. As we waited, I pulled a book out of the book bag that I had brought with me. I opened it to a "random" page, which I often do, and my eyes fell on the following Bible verse.

Ephesians 6:5-7 "Slaves, be obedient to those who are your masters according to the flesh, with fear and trembling, in the sincerity of your heart, as to Christ; not by way of eyeservice, as men-pleasers, but as slaves of Christ, doing the will of God from the heart. With good will render service, as to the Lord, and not to men." The footnote of the author of the book paraphrased the verse by saying, "Even if you are coerced into doing something; do everything as a service to the Lord." After I read that verse from Ephesians, I felt a calmness come over me that proved to be my saving grace.

God had used this verse to command me to obey Him.

It certainly was not my idea to be there. I definitely did feel coerced because it was not a volunteer event. But I had a healthy fear of God and my conscience would not allow me to lie my way out of it. Also, I truly was grateful that the judicial system had worked for my family all those years ago.

When the time was right all forty-five of us were told to enter the courtroom. We raised our hands and swore to tell the truth when asked questions about ourselves and to obey the laws of the land. I agreed with that premise, but I knew I was really answerable to a higher power, my God and Savior Jesus Christ.

I will not go into every detail, but I will say that I was called to be one of 40 people to sit in the front of the court room. We answered some basic questions about ourselves. After this time called voir dire, the judge revealed the facts of the case. It was, in fact, a murder trial. I had been brought face to face with a most dreaded situation. What happened next was even more shocking. The judge proceeded to announce facts surrounding the murder.

He announced the name of the accused man, <u>who was sitting beside his attorney</u>, and the name of the murdered man. I could barely believe what I heard. The murdered man's name was almost identical to the name of the man that had killed my parents. It was so similar that in this situation I could not hear the slight difference except that this man was a junior. My mind raced. Could this be his son? I grabbed the sides of the chair I was sitting in to calm myself. The whole thing seemed surreal. After we had been given permission to leave for lunch and instructions about what to do when we returned, I went up to one of the stenographers and told her briefly my concern. If this was his son, they needed to know about my connection to him. The stenographer recounted my words to the judge. He asked me to wait until the other potential jurors had left and then he asked me to repeat what I had just told the stenographer. The judge, stenographers, lawyers, and the accused man were there when I said aloud to everyone in the room that 38 years ago my parents had been murdered by a man with the same name as the murdered man and I did not know for sure if he had a son or not. The judge asked me if I could be fair and impartial as a juror. My answer was "yes" because I had come to peace about the way my parents had died. Then I said that on the way to my parent's funeral the thought came to my mind that if the man who killed them repented of his sins my parents would welcome him into heaven someday. The judge looked at me with a shocked look on his face. Then I added that the system had worked for my family and I was grateful for that. The judge asked me to step outside the courtroom while he, the prosecuting attorney and the defense attorney discussed whether to dismiss me or not. The bailiff led me to the hall to wait again. The judge's instructions had been to decide the case based on the evidence and the law without "passion and prejudice." (I found out later that when a potential juror has had a life experience closely resembling the facts of the case that person will likely be excused by the court.) I stood there awaiting their decision. The bailiff came back in a few minutes to tell me to come inside the court room. The judge spoke to me and said that I might be better suited for another case. I was free to go. Of course, I was relieved. It was clear that in God's providence I had not been summoned to sit on the jury to decide this man's fate, but I was summoned by the highest of all powers to "testify" to the forgiveness available to every sinner. I had submitted to the Father, and He had given me the words He wanted me to say.

Just think about it, out of thousands of eligible people my name had been chosen "randomly" for the murder trial of a man whose name very closely resembled the name of the man who had killed my parents. I opened the book "randomly" that had been given to me at a garage sale a couple of weeks earlier but had not read before that day. The excerpt I read that day from the book spoke to me of God's command to obey Him willingly and from my heart.

I think it is noteworthy to state that the date of my "testimony" was on September 11, 2018. On September 11th, 2001 terrorist attacked America. The 9-11 attack was a warning of impending judgement on our nation. We have had time to repent of our many national sins and receive forgiveness. Taking the life of the unborn is a murder that is legal in our society but abhorrent to our God. The terrorist knew that dialing 911 on a phone was symbolic of the summoning of emergency personnel. Since none of us knows how long we have on this planet God's call for repentance is urgent. The accused man was found guilty and sentenced to many years in prison. He has time to contemplate his deeds and recon himself worthy of judgement, crushed with guilt, and cry out for forgiveness or to ignore the plan of salvation available to all sinners.

All I can say is that someone must have prayed for him. I was stunned and humbled to be used by God in this way.

At the age of 68 I am now one of the older generations. I can testify to the mighty hand of God's love and protection. My inheritance is the call to stand in the gap between God and man, persist in prayer, and realize that He is all around us. He invited me to enter in the wrestling match. I had wrestled with God over the possibility of being a juror. God had won and I was blessed in the process. I realize that I do not deserve forgiveness any more than the man who sat in that court room and heard those words. The free book is also symbolic of the free gift of God's forgiveness available to all of us.

Jesus Testified to His Deity

In the third chapter of the book of John a man named Nicodemus questioned Jesus. Nicodemus was a Pharisee, as such he had authority in the temple and prestige in the Jewish community. He came to Jesus after dark and began a dialogue. The voir dire in a court means to "speak the truth" when asked questions about yourself. Jesus did just that. Jurors are not accused of wrongdoing, but they are questioned as to their willingness to be truthful about themselves. And they are judged as to their qualifications to serve.

Jesus has been proven to be qualified to serve as our Savior.

In God's order of things and at the end of His brief life on earth Jesus <u>was</u> accused of wrongdoing. He was publicly accused of claiming He was God. He did not speak in His own defense in a court of human law. But in a one-on one encounter with Nicodemus He allowed Himself to be questioned. He spoke the truth and His answers are some of the most profound words ever spoken.

When He was accused of wrong doing the people of that day acted as judge, jury and executioner. Jesus temporarily put aside His judicial responsibilities. And while He appeared to be submitting to the desires of the mob, He really was submitting to God the Father's plan for our redemption. And remember Jesus had the final last word when He came back to life after suffering and dying for our sins. Please do not misunderstand. He will someday judge the world for the unrighteous deeds done.

. . . The Lord is our judge, the Lord is our lawyer, the Lord is our King. He will save us. Isaiah 33:22

But when He was walking this earth He came to suffer, and to die for our sin. He is rose from the dead and He is alive and well. Right now, He is sitting at the right hand of God the Father. He interceded for us on the cross and He intercedes for us now because he asked the Father not to take us out of this world, but to keep us from the evil one. (Hebrews 7:25 and John 17:15-17 my paraphrase)

THE STORY OF NICODEMUS

John 3:1-16

Now there was a man of the Pharisees, named Nicodemus, a ruler of the Jews; this man came to Him by night, and said to Him, Rabbi, we know that you have come from God as a teacher; for no one can do these signs that You do unless God is with him." Jesus answered and said to him,

"Truly. Truly, I say to you, unless one is born again, he cannot see the kingdom of God." Nicodemus said to Him, "How can a man be born when he is old? He cannot enter a second time into his mother's womb and be born, can he? Jesus answered, **"Truly, truly I say to you, unless one is born of the Spirit, he cannot enter the kingdom of God.** That which is born of the flesh is flesh, and that which is born of the Spirit is spirit . . . . Nicodemus answered and said to Him, "How can these things be?" Jesus answered and said to him, "Are you the teacher of Israel, and do not understand these things? **"Truly, truly, I say to you, we speak that which we know, and bear witness of that which we have seen; and you do not receive our witness.** "If I told you earthly things and you do not believe, how shall you believe if I tell you heavenly things? "And no one has ascended into heaven, but He who descended from heaven, even the Son of Man. "And as Moses lifted up the serpent in the wilderness, even so must the Son of Man be lifted up; that whoever believes in Him have eternal life.

For God so lived the world, that He gave His only begotten Son,
that whosoever believes in Him should not perish but have eternal life.

Jesus repeated the word "truly" six times. I believe He wanted to emphasize that He was speaking the truth and to proclaim that there is no self-styled way of coming to God. The Father had a plan that would assure our ability to be born again. He used the example of the days of Moses when a bronze serpent was placed at the top of a pole providing a healing opportunity for the people of that day. It was a story that Nicodemus would have been very familiar with. Jesus was telling Nicodemus that He would have to be lifted up or crucified for the healing of our sin sick souls.

EACH OF US MUST BE CRUCIFIED

Paul said, "I have been crucified with Christ; it is no longer I who live, but Christ lives in me; and the life which I now live in the flesh I live by faith in the Son of God, who loved Me and gave Himself for me." Galatians 2:20

I take a moment now to pray for the family of the murdered man. I know that for them it is really never over. I pray that the man found guilty of murder admits that he is a sinner. May his confession lead to repentance. Lord, help him see that even though his physical body is in prison his spirit can be free. Please give him purpose and gratitude for all You have done. Lord, I thank you. I was honored to testify to an encounter I had with You all those years ago. I was blessed to be used by you and I thank You that my stressed-out disposition was changed. You are the composer and conductor of our lives. I played my instrument that day because your power gave me a voice to speak the truth about the availability of forgiveness. I needed a touch of the Potter. You had broken me of feeling distressed and intimidated in an extremely uncomfortable situation. In the process You molded me to Your will in a way that nothing else could have.

GOD'S DESIRE FOR US TURNED INTO A PRAYER REQUEST:

Adapted from Deuteronomy 5:29

"Oh, that we would have such a heart in us that we would fear God,
and keep all His commandments always,
and that it may be well with us and with our children forever"
Amen and Amen!

Bible verses referenced:

Two men on the road to Emmaus – Luke 24:13-35

A call to obedience – Ephesians 6:5-7

Daddy's favorite Bible verse, "I sought for a man among them, that should make up the hedge, and stand in the gap before Me for the land." Ezekiel 22:30

God's words to the older generation – Deuteronomy 11:2-11

Jacob wrestled with God – Genesis 32:22-32

We are all sinners in need of God's forgiveness – Isaiah 53:6

Jesus is our Judge, Lawyer, King and our Savior - Isaiah 33:22

Jesus is our intercessor - Hebrews 7:25

He asked that the Father leave us in this world and protect us – John 17:15-17

The story of Nicodemus – John 3:1-16

Life lived by faith in God – Galatians 2:20

We are the clay, and He is the Potter – Isaiah 64:8 and Romans 9:19-29

God's desire for us – Deuteronomy 5:29

CHAPTER 9

HINDRANCES TO FELLOWSHIP WITH OUR LORD — MISPLACED FEAR

Fear of the Lord leads to Life. Fear of life leads to distrust of the Lord.

"The fear of the Lord is the beginning of wisdom."
Psalms 111:10

"For as high as the heavens are above the earth, so great is His lovingkindness toward those who fear Him. As far as the east is from the west, so far has He removed our transgressions from us. Just as a father has compassion on his children, so the Lord has compassion on those who fear Him. For He Himself knows our frame; He is mindful that we are but dust." Psalms 103:11-14

He is not mad at us. His righteous anger was satisfied because Jesus bore the punishment for our sin.

There is an enormous difference between reverential awe with trust and the kind of fear that prompts us to distrust the God who loves us so.

FEARS LEADING TO DISTRUST

If fear of life is the primary symptom of unbelief, then blessed change can only come as we face our fears.

The very first thing that needs to change is the misconception that we *can* change ourselves.

The true revelation is that we are **not to live a life focused on change** but instead are to live **an exchanged life**.

HIS LIFE EXCHANGED FOR OURS

While our sin is forgiven, old behavior patterns, habits and attitudes still remain, and it is the work of the Holy Spirit to reveal to us where we are in need of spiritual cleansing and healing. Our dispositions need exchanging; that is, the way we look at life needs to be aligned with His way.

In my own life fear became a constant companion. Without realizing it I was submitting to an evil spirit that was determined to undo me. For me, fear was the primary manifestation of not believing that God is who He says He is. I suspect the same is true for all of us. Fearfulness may show itself by any number of behaviors. The end result is the same; eyes focused on self are not focused on God and His blessed presence that comforts us.

Of what are we most afraid?

For most of us it is probably relinquishing control to a God we cannot see.

The Bible says, "Blessed are they who did not see, yet believed." John 20:29

"Things which are seen are temporal, but the things which are not seen are eternal." 2 Corinthians 4: 18

Our human tendency is to try and find a list of behaviors that we think we can adhere to and set about to follow that list. It seems like surrender when in fact we are not surrendering to God's plan and relinquishing control; instead we are setting ourselves up as the master of our fate.

"Do you not know that your body is a temple of the Holy Spirit who is in you, whom you have from God, and that you are not your own? For

you have been bought with a price, therefore glorify God in your body."
1 Corinthians 6: 19-20

I must not lay claim to myself. There was a price to pay for that. What was the price? Years of futile searching for something outside myself when the Holy Spirit was there within me all along. Good works do not save a person but are evidence of an exchanged life. Relationship with God produces works worthy to proclaim, "He is risen, and He is Lord!"

When a gunman kills someone it is said, "He claimed the life of the person."

Likewise, when someone lies for the purpose of destroying a person's reputation, we call that character assassination.

I submit to you that rejecting Christ as the Savior and trying to save ourselves is spiritual suicide.

So, what do we, the already saved, have to do with eternal spiritual death? NOTHING!

He came to give us abundant LIFE.

A biblical paradox is a tenant that seems contradictory to common sense, but yet, is true.

The paradox is this –

To have the abundant life that Christ has made available to us we must die daily to self. It is as simple as an honest seeking prayer.

Michael Wells put it this way:

"My only responsibility is to abide. Everything else makes life difficult."
To that I say a resounding AMEN!

What use is there to be "like" a walking dead person when Jesus has made a way to satisfy the Father's requirement of holiness? Only the sinless Son of God could do it and only the Father's love for us could cause goodness to come from such a wonderfully terrible event as the crucifixion of our Lord. When we Christians lay claim to ourselves, we are in opposition to the God we say we love. Nothing short of surrender will satisfy the true longing of our heart. And nothing except denial of self will satisfy the flesh of man.

Holiness defined: Our soul is not made righteous. It does become holy as we obey Gods' word. It is our spirit that is declared righteous when we trust Jesus as our savior.

Our Savior did not lay claim to Himself but gave Himself up for us all. One of my husband's favorite verses is Matthew 26:53 , when Jesus told Peter that He could call twelve legions of angels to rescue Him from impending death. (my paraphrase)

"The Father loves Me, because I lay down My life that I may take it again. No one has taken it away from Me, because I lay it down on my own initiative, I have authority to lay it down, and I have authority to take it up again. This commandment I received from My Father." John 10:17-18

Since the enemy of our souls cannot have us for eternity, he will do all he can to steal our joy, kill our witness and destroy our character. Whether we want to admit it or not we are in a war.

"The thief comes only to steal, kill and destroy; I (Jesus) came that they might have life, and might have it abundantly." John 10:10

So, when we lay claim to ourselves, we are playing right into the enemy's hands.

Let's think back to the woman at the well, the two on the road to Emmaus and the story of the two daughters. The people in these stories were perplexed but not despairing.

Paul said, "We are afflicted in every way, but not crushed, perplexed but not despairing." If the apostle Paul found himself perplexed, we should not be surprised when it happens to us.

> Being perplexed can be a very valuable emotion
> if it leads us to seek The Truth.

M. Scott Peck a noted psychologist and believer in Jesus Christ made the following observations:

"There are four basic stages of spiritual growth. We do not move smoothly from one stage to the other. We go back and forth a lot." Sometimes we get stuck in one of the stages.

Peck's stages are listed below:

Stage 1 is chaos.

Stage 2 people are <u>un</u>comfortable with things that are not cut-and-dried. They like formal institutional boundaries like prison/military/ business corporations/church. Stage 2 people get very upset if rituals are changed. They have very little idea that God lives inside us. (Immanent – the dwelling divinity within the human spirit) They need a benevolent cop kind of God. They are glad to be liberated from the chaos of stage 1.

Stage 3 people are skeptic individuals who are truth seekers. If they seek truth deeply enough and widely enough they do fit enough pieces of the truth together to get glimpses of the big picture and see that it is not only very beautiful, but strangely resembles many of the principles that stage 2 parents embraced.

Stage 4 people could be described as "mystical/communal." They see cohesion beneath the surface of things and are comfortable with mystery, they even love it. (End of quote)

To be perplexed with life isn't sin. It's called being human.

If people passing through stage 3 are honest in their skepticism; God will break them of the obsession with their stage 2 self. Contained within all of us are traces of all four stages and we can revert at any time.

HE WILL BREAK TO BLESS

There is a whole collection of hyphenated self-sins. The predominate one being that of approaching God in a self-styled way.

Jesus said, "I am the way, the truth, and the life, no one comes to the Father except by Me." John 14:6

The list goes on to self-sufficiency, self-pity, self-protection, self-indulgent tenderness, self-centeredness, self-destructiveness, self-serving . . . You get the idea!

Try as we may, self will never get better. It's not supposed to get better. It's supposed to get weaker.

Paul said, "He (the Lord) has said to me, "My grace is sufficient for you, for power is perfected in weakness. Most gladly, therefore, I will rather boast about my weaknesses, that the power of Christ may dwell in me. Therefore, I am well content with weaknesses, with insults, with distresses, with persecutions, with difficulties. For when I am weak, then I am strong." 2 Corinthians 12:9-10

(My paraphrase) When we are weak in (self-strength) our spirit becomes strong in the Lord's strength.

Here is where choice comes in.

We are either nourishing the old self nature or nourishing the life of Christ in us. The one we choose to feed is the one that will grow.

The life of Christ in us will suffer if we do not pray. Prayer is the only way to get in touch with Reality. It's to bad we often wait until we come to our wits end.

Ps. 107: 27-28 : "They were at their wits' end, then they cried to the Lord in their trouble, and He brought them out of their distresses."

There is a saying going around these days that pronounces that, "perception becomes reality." I know what they mean. Our attitudes about life are influenced by prevailing beliefs in society. But that saying is false. The truth is, "Perception becomes <u>perceived</u> reality." No wonder our society is swimming in chaos. God is Reality and He never changes.

The Law of Moses was never intended to save the people. God gave them rituals that covered their sin for a year and pictured the substitutional death of Christ. Today, most Jews don't even follow all the ceremonial laws but we Christians must be careful that we do not proceed to set up new laws and try to combine them with Grace.

GOD'S GRACE AND MAN-MADE LAW CAN NEVER BE COMBINED – THEY ARE OPPOSITES

Grace says: "Salvation is a free gift from God." Our laws say, "You must work to obtain salvation.

Grace says: "God loves you and Jesus died for you." Our law appeals to our FEAR OF FAILURE and says: "Love God or suffer consequences."

Grace says: "I, The Lord will put a new heart in you." Our law appeals to our PERFECTIONISM and says: "Change your own heart and get it right."

Grace says: "You are forgiven." Our law appeals to our PRIDE and says: "Forgiveness is earned."

Grace says: "You can never save yourself. You need Me." Our law appeals to our sense of FAIRNESS and says: "You can save yourself if you obey a list of "good" behaviors."

Grace says: "Jesus is the only way to the Father. "Our law appeals to our SELF-STYLED approach to God and says: "You can do it your way."

Grace says: "I owe you nothing; yet I give you everything pertaining to life and godliness. "Our law appeals to our CONTRACT STATE OF MIND and says: "God you owe me. My work deserves a living wage."

If the wage of sin is death, then the wage of legalism is sin leading to spiritual death. The very thing we don't want to do is the very thing we find ourselves doing. (Romans 7:15-20 paraphrased)

So, what is the purpose of the Law? The Law of God shows us that morality is not relative. And its purpose is to show us that without God we are doomed to walk according to the flesh and be dominated by our sin nature as long as we live. It proves to us that we are in desperate need of the Savior.

Grace saves and gives us the motivation and power to live the way God wants us to live. We are already acceptable to Him. So, we can walk on with Him down any road He chooses, witness to others and accumulate the rewards God rejoices to give us when we see Him in heaven.

M. Scott Peck was right when he said that we do a lot of vacillating in our spiritual growth. But as we begin to grasp the vastness of our sin nature and get a glimpse of what life in God can be like other fears will emerge. One by one those fears will fall by the side of the roadway as we walk and talk with the Savior's Spirit. He will explain precious truths to us.

Dear Lord, please help us remember and bring to our minds the truth that we deserve to die for our sin. Our holy occupation is to be obsessed with You. If we have committed our lives to You; prayer becomes our "dream job." Repentance is a way of life and joy displaces fear of failure. To rest and work at the same time seems imposable to our mortal minds. Show us the way to peace that passes all understanding.

THE MISPLACED FEAR OF MISSING GOD'S GUIDANCE

Decisions – Decisions – Decisions

We have established that one of the Holy Spirit's jobs is to lead us in the ways of the Lord and give us wisdom to make wise decisions. It is not enough to believe in Jesus, we must get to know Him. Our daily decisions are fertile ground for learning to abide/remain in His presence. We are told to pray without ceasing. We can't sit with our hands pressed together in prayer and get anything done. To be sure those quiet times are precious to our Lord, but He wants us to walk with Him and talk to Him as we go through life.

I once heard a friend say that she had been distressed about which college her daughter would attend. The Lord spoke to her heart and said, "The thing that matters is that I have her heart."

If the daughter let Him lead her, she would end up where she belonged. But often we are either willful and want something other than God's will, we don't know how to ask, seek, and knock or we mistake God's will for that of other people. But He is greater than our decisions and He will go with us wherever we go.

In the parable of the Sower, our Lord teaches us that God's loving kindnesses are falling all around us. Within each seed is the potential for a blessing. We must partner with Him and let Him lead us in doing our part. He does the miraculous which only He can do. I believe the four grounds are within all of us and match beautifully with the four stages of spiritual growth that M. Scott Peck describes.

The Sower Sows the Word

Mark 4:4-20

Jesus said, **"LISTEN TO THIS!** The Sower went out to sow. Some seed fell beside the road and birds came and ate it up." This is an example of people who hear the word but immediately Satan comes and takes it away. The word, which was sown in them produces no stability, only chaos.

It's not much different for the seed sown on the rocky places. "These are like the people who hear the word and immediately receive it with joy, but they have no firm root in themselves." The benefit is only temporary because "when affliction or persecution arises, they fell away." These are the ones who have erected a God in their own image. Their preconceived ideas of what life in God is supposed to look like is in opposition to the plans He has for them. They seek out boundaries that give them a temporary feeling of security. This could be anything from street gangs to institutional ritualistic churches. The rituals will vary dramatically but the purpose is the same. The purpose is to keep the God they cannot control as far away as possible. Certainty in our beliefs creates uncertainty in God.

Notice, the Sower persists. He does not stop even when the seeds fall among the thorns. "The thorns came up and choked it yielding no crop." These people are skeptical about God. The things the world has to offer sound much better. When worries come, riches disappoint and bring emptiness; the Word of God seems even less relevant. This is where decisions come in to play. They can allow the world, the flesh and the devil to **press them into God** and plow the ground for "stage four" or they can allow difficulties to harden their hearts even more. But if they come to their wits end and cry out, "Abba, Father," their soil becomes fertile with the potential of reconciliation with the Sower the and fruits of His Spirit immerge from the earth that was barren. He is with us through every "stage." It is as if, in His humility, He says, "If this is what you give Me, this is what I'll work with."

PRESSURE POEM:

Pressed out of measure
Pressed to all length
Pressed so intently it seems beyond strength
Pressed in the body
Pressed in the soul
Pressed in the mind
Till the dark surges roll

Pressure by foes and
Pressure by friends
Pressure on pressure till life nearly ends

Pressed into knowing no helper but God
Pressed into loving the staff and the rod
Pressed into liberty where nothing clings
Pressed into faith for impossible things

Pressed into living a life in the Lord
Pressed into living a Christ life outpoured. By Annie Johnson Flint
Certainty in God produces peace that passes all understanding.
LISTEN TO THIS!

God loves you. He will not leave you. He will complete
the work He has begun. And He will even prepare you
for the emotional pain that surely will come.

LISTEN TO THIS!

His mercies are new every morning,
Great is His faithfulness. Amen (So it will be)

THE MISPLACED FEAR OF EMOTIONAL PAIN

Because of the violent nature of my parents' death I feared more devastating emotional pain. Self-protection became a goal of my life. I laid claim to myself and suffered the consequences. When we worry, we get what we deserve – more worry. I fed my fears and they consumed me. I found myself overmuch dwelling on the uncertainties of life and imagining that things will inevitably work out for the worst. I dwelt on my helplessness. The consequences were that worry, and fear bred more worry and more fear. A series of thought patterns emerged. But our loving God constitutes things in such a way that for a child of God everything works to bless us. He is right there waiting for us to be ready for new revelation of who He is.

There are many, many things of which we are helpless to change but we need not ever abide (remain) in a hopeless state of mind.

"Fear NOT for I am with you: do not look anxiously about you, surely I will help you, surely I will uphold you with My righteous right hand." Is. 41:10

The words "Fear not" spoken to our heart by God mean this:

Receive the courage My Spirit imparts
and receive the power to follow through to freedom.

I will tell you a little story from my own life that addresses helplessness and hopelessness. My husband and I had two adorable Scottish terrier dogs. Maggie lived to be 12 years old and Max to almost 14. The day after Max died, I was very sad and crying to the Lord. God spoke these words to my heart. He said, "They were guests in your home for a very long time but now it is time for them to leave." I already knew that information. It was not a new concept but when the Holy Spirit speaks words, those words come with power to save. He helped me see that while I was helpless to add a single day to Max's life, I had hope in my Lord to brighten my day.

The truth is that God already sees us exactly the way we are. No one knows human nature like God knows human nature. He sees our sin as a potential catalyst for the exchange that only He can accomplish. We are helpless to change ourselves, but we need not ever be hopeless for very long.

"When my anxious thoughts multiply within me Thy consolations delight my soul." (mind, will and emotions) Psalm 94:19

HERE ARE A FEW CONSOLATIONS:

Philippians 4:6--8	Isaiah 57:18	Isaiah 66:13
Psalms 55:22	2 Corinthians 13:4	2 Corinthians 9:8
Colossians 3:15-16	1 Corinthians 16:13	Psalms 96
2 Timothy 1:7	Psalms 100	2 Timothy 1:8-9

THE MISPLACED FEAR OF LOOSING IDENTITY

Some of the most seemingly self-assured people I know have the most fragile self-image. They will go to great lengths to protect themselves from being found out a phony. If you have been caught in their wake you know what I mean. If I have just described you then know this - there is no sin that has overtaken you that the Spirit of God has not seen before, and His arm is not too short to save.

C.S. Lewis said that the prayer proceeding all prayer is this:

"May it be the real I who speaks,
"May it be the real Thou that I speak to."

We just do not realize that the real desire of our heart is to embrace our true identity in Christ. He created each of us to be a unique expression of Himself. "In Him we live and move and have our being."

And remember, just as the human physical heart has many chambers; it takes many spiritual changes of heart to come to places of peace.

I want to share with you the closest I have come to recording a change of my heart.

This is a prayer journal entry from several years ago.

Dear Lord, a few days ago I asked You to help me understand why I am so fearful. Please help me understand the story of Gideon and his soldiers; all but 300 were sent back because they were afraid.

They were afraid to enter into battle because they could die.

Thank You for helping me understand myself and my fear.

I am afraid to enter into battle with the enemy because my flesh will be revealed in the process and I will be called to die to things I have clung to for so long. When confronted with difficult circumstances, self rises up OR I abide in Your presence and experience death to self. It feels scary like I don't recognize this person – seems unfamiliar - the unknown (like death). Don't panic. Don't look for a way to avoid it. Temptation is not sin. Deliverance is near. Victory is at hand. Little victories lead to more victory. Amen

The Holy Spirit wants to guide, comfort and teach us the truth about ourselves. He will chasten us for our good and He will show us that maintaining control of our lives is an illusion anyway. Trying to maintain control is not worth the trouble it affords us. He will break us only to bless us. And, when we are ready, He will deliver us from all our fears and give us the spiritual fruit of self-control.

"I sought the Lord and He answered me, and
delivered me from all my fears." Psalms 34:4
"I fear no evil; for Thou art with me." Ps. 23:4
Praise God from whom all blessings flow, Praise
Him all you creatures here below,
Praise Father, Son, and Holy Ghost. Amen

THE MISPLACED FEAR OF NOT HAVING REALLY REPENTED

Another Hinderance To Fellowship with Our Lord
I think the cycle of slavery to sin goes something like this-
Repent, repent, and repent without rejoicing.
Then . . ., repent in advance of stumbling.
(Would be better to worship and rejoice in advance of stumbling).
Instead of gratitude for our Lord having taken the sins
away; we tend to review past failures and either
repent again or assume failure will inevitably come.
A person in this cycle is blind to the concept that
temptation is not sin.
Only worship will break the cycle of bondage to sin.

The apostle Paul admits to the struggle within himself. He talks about the disposition of sin deep in his life that produces sinful acts.

"For the good that I wish, I do not do; but I practice the very evil that I do not wish. But if I am doing the very thing I do not wish, I am no longer the one doing it, but sin which dwells in me." Romans 7:19-20

The person dominated by sin endures a "living" death.

"Wretched man that I am! Who will set me free from the body of this death? Thanks be to God through Jesus Christ our Lord!" (Romans 7:19-20, 24-25A)

"For you have <u>not</u> received a spirit of **slavery** leading to fear again, but you have received a spirit of adoption as sons by which we cry out, "Abba! Father!" (Romans 8:15)

The following Michael Wells quotation is the best description of true repentance I have ever come across.

Michael Wells asked the question, "Are you certain you want to be free?"

"If you do want to be free pray this prayer."

"Lord, apart from You I can do nothing; today I give You _____ , and **I thank YOU** that no matter what, You have taken it."

"What is needed is the supernatural action of God that comes only when we have our eyes off the problem and on Him through abiding."

THE MISPLACED FEAR OF FAILING TO JUDGE PROPERLY

One More Hinderance To Fellowship
Comparing Ourselves with Other People

I have learned much from our brother in Christ Michael Wells. He said, "God's glory is revealed in contrast. If God sent His Son for the sinless, we would think very little of His love, but since He sent His Son for sinners, we note the vast expanse between His glory and sinners and begin to comprehend how great His love is."

As we observe differences, we learn so much!
Contrast   vs.   Comparing

Contrast as a noun means to observe differences. Comparing is a verb only. It is a word of action.

It seems to me that comparing is a more personal endeavor. Our sin nature always wants to know how we are doing and if we are ahead of others or falling behind. Competition soon follows. Someone said, "Competition is deadly to relationships." That is because it causes disunity even between Christ's followers. Galatians 5:26 "Let us not become boastful, challenging one another, envying one another."

COMPARING CAN BE JUDGEMENTAL WHILE OBSERVING CONTRASTS CAN BE PAINFUL.

I once observed a woman about my age thoroughly enjoying interaction with her two little granddaughters. In that moment I was brought face to face with the longing of my heart to hug my granddaughters who live a distance from us. I wanted to laugh with them and enjoy their sweet presence. I had not sought out this observation nor did I judge her in any way; the contrast was unavoidable. The Lord does not spare us from all our pain. But He does say that He will comfort us in all our sorrows. He reminded me that she has her own losses and her own pain that I have no business knowing about. His grace is sufficient for me and the challenges He gives me. The same is true for her if she seeks Him with all our heart. As I write these words, I find myself praying for her.

Oswald Chambers said, "If through a broken heart God can bring His purposes to pass in the world, then thank Him for breaking your heart."

Dear Lord, when I observe contrasts in the lives of your children
I can choose to rejoice in the clarity your
revelation brings and stand against
the temptation to bow a knee to any spirit other than Your own.

The enemy of our soul's desires to reward our comparing by feeding the desire in us to take a contrast, compare ourselves with others and say to ourselves, "Aren't I wonderful" or "Poor me!"

So, in this fallen world, how are we Christians to face the problem in relation to observable contrasts? We aren't quite sure what to do with the information. Often, we rush to make judgements and end up criticizing God for allowing the pain. Or we criticize other people for not behaving in a way we approve of. God's word tells us, "Judge not lest you be judged." Matthew 7:1

So again, how do we navigate a world that requires us to make judgements without passing judgement on others? We are required to make moral distinctions lest we are so passive that we call evil good and good evil. Isaiah 5:20-21 "Woe to those who call evil good and good evil, who substitutes darkness for light and light for darkness."

God reminded me of a bit of trivia from my years teaching elementary school. The first seven state of being verbs are: is, are, was, were, be, being and been. It helps me to think that when my born-again spirit aligns with God, I do not want to compare myself with others and "be" judgmental. I don't want to hang out there, get comfortable and assume that my observations are always accurate. In every circumstance there is much I have no way of knowing. I don't want my disposition (the way I look at the world) to be that of a fault finder.

Instead of "being" judgmental I can choose to; "Be still and know that He is God." Psalm 46:10

In that quiet place near to the heart of God
I find compassion and peace.

It takes an act of the will to remain still and in the experienced will of God. That kind of stillness does not equate to inactivity. But the actions will not be frantic or look to other humans for validation. We will still observe the contrasts and will be challenged to wait for our Sovereign Lord to reveal our response.

As we reside in the state of abiding God gives wisdom. Decisions and attitudes are based on His guidance and obedience is on the basis of His leading.

In that blessed "state of being" we will have joys, comforts and sorrows. The sorrows will bring us low and humble us. God desires to be the Lifter of our heads. (Ps. 3:36) as we proclaim, "He is Almighty God and His counsel is wonderful!"

Is. 9:6 "His name will be called Wonderful Counselor, Mighty God."

So, the challenge of living in a fallen world of contrasts presses me into the abiding relationship and as Michael Wells would say, "God's mission is accomplished in my life."

Lord may the state of our being harmonize with our calling.
Let our light so shine as to contrast with the
darkness and draw all men to YOU. Amen

Matthew 5:16 "Let your light shine before men in such a way that they may see your good works and glorify your Father who is in heaven."

THE MISPLACED FEAR OF NOT GETTING
WHAT WE WANT - WHEN WE WANT IT

The story of Lazarus is an example of the principles of wanting something desperately and being required to wait.

"Now a certain man was sick, Lazarus of Bethany." John 11:1

Lazarus was a man dearly loved by his two sisters Mary and Martha. Jesus had spent much time with them in their home. He loved them and they loved Him in return. When their brother became very ill, they sent word to Jesus. "Lord, behold he whom thou lovest is sick." John 11:3

Jesus' reply was perplexing to them. He said, "This sickness is not unto death, but for the glory of God, that the Son of God Might be glorified thereby." John 11:4

"He stayed for two days in the town where He was at the time." John 11:6

Jesus said it was not a sickness unto death and then Lazarus died.

I think He wanted the sisters to reach a place of helplessness. Sometimes He waits until we are convinced that it is too late and impossible. There are always reasons for God's actions. Often God's closest children are sorely tested. When He does answer; all doubt is erased as to who gave deliverance and the Son of God does get the glory.

"Then Jesus said plainly (to the disciples), "Lazarus is dead, and I am glad for your sakes that I was not there, **so that you may believe**; but let us go to him." John 11:14-15 (Emphases added)

No one wants problems. We want life to be easy, problem free and we want it our way. We want God to resolve all our problems. He wants to give us the resolve to trust Him when problems persist or even, in our opinion, get worse.

It is important to remember this:

"He only permits wounding that accelerates our ending well. And He only prevents things that would hinder that same ending." Michael Wells

"God permits what He hates in order to bring about what He loves." Joni Erickson Tada quote

Could it be that Lazarus' death and soon resurrection pictured Jesus' own impending death and resurrection? When Lazarus' family grieved their loss it sounds a lot like His words to the disciples in John 16:20 when he said, "Truly, truly, I say to you, that you will weep and lament, but the world will rejoice; you will be sorrowful, but your sorrow will be turned to joy."

Jesus told them very clearly that Lazarus's death was for their benefit; so that they would believe. Believe what? I think He wanted them to believe that He meant it when He said He would die, the world would rejoice, and they would mourn His passing. He wanted them to anticipate the joy they would experience when He was resurrected.

When He saw the people weeping, Jesus was deeply moved. He wept. (John 11: 33-35). We can only speculate as to the exact reasons for His distress. Was He grieved for Lazarus' family? Was He sad because of the sinful condition of the world that leads to sickness and death or was He grieved because they didn't really believe Him when He said it was not a sickness unto death? Perhaps He thought of His own mother; if the Spirit reminded Him of the words spoken to Mary by Simeon when she brought Him to the temple for His firstborn sacrifice.

"Behold, this child is appointed for the fall and rise of many in Israel and for a sign to be opposed. A sword will pierce even your own soul (Mary) to the end that thoughts from many hearts may be revealed." Luke 2:34-35

Father God would not spare His only Son the sword that would pierce His side, nor would He spare Mary the sword of agony that would pierce her soul when she witnessed Jesus' death.

This one thing we know for sure: weeping was part of His nature and it will be part of ours too.

Jesus, the God Man, could perfectly identify with the pain of His human family and the pain of His Father-God. We humans struggle to have the mind of Christ. When we begin to think His thoughts after Him, He will impoverish the self that is set against Him by taking us through times of sorrow that have a blessedness about them. There in that blessed place we learn to be helpless and hopeful at the same time.

When our hope is reduced to Jesus only, we can ask whatever we will because we are convinced that He knows best and has our best in mind.

Often a puzzling thing happens. God sometimes answers our prayers in a way that tests His righteousness in our eyes. You see He never becomes a tame lion. The Lion of Judea does as He pleases. Our only responsibility is to abide (remain in his <u>experienced</u> presence), believe Him and trust Him.

Then we can truly say and mean it when we say; "**<u>I have Jesus. He is all I need.</u>**"

The Bible says that He stores our tears in a bottle. (Psalms 56:8) Only precious things are kept. Worthless things are thrown away. Our Lord never wastes our afflictions.

"He does not afflict willingly." Lamentations 3:33

"It was good that I was afflicted that I may learn Thy statues." Psalm 119:71 ()

> "My troubles turned out all for the best – they
> forced me to learn from Your textbook.
> Truth from Your mouth means more to me
> than striking it rich in a gold mine."
> Psalm 119:71-72 <u>The Message</u>

Gratitude does take on many forms. One of which is acknowledging that God does have our best interest in His mind and that our afflictions will work to bless us in ways we never could have imagined.

> "Few delights equal the mere presence of One
> we trust utterly." George McDonald

Lazarus did come back to life but not until the time the Father had chosen in order to bring glory to the Son and attest to His true identity.

In the affairs of men our God is Sovereign. He is in control. He can do anything. He controls everything and He does what He knows is best.

Fear is a powerful motivator. It will either work to bless us if we let God show us the way through our dark night of the soul or it will be a stumbling block and a hindrance.

His Sovereignty should calm our fears and protect us from the temptation to sin.

A simple definition of sin is doing life my way and not God's way. When the Israelis where standing at the Red Sea with the Egyptian army bearing down behind them and an impassable body of water ahead of them Moses uttered these reassuring words; "The Lord will fight for you, you need only to be still and wait." In Hebrew the word for "be still" is translated "to let go, to release."

I have found in my own life that God often wants me to be willing to hear Him say "NO" to my request. Then, when I have let go and released my will, He often allows me to do what I wanted to do in the first place. This letting go attitude is not passivity. It is an active decision to acknowledge that God is in control. "Be still and know that I am God." Psalm 46:10

Mary and Martha were required to release their brother's body, soul and spirit into the hands of the Father. Jesus delay left no doubt in anyone's mind that Lazarus was gone on to be with the Father, but the story did not end there.

We started this section of the book with the fear of relinquishing control of our life to a God we cannot see and we are ending it with the fear of not getting what we want when we want it. Sounds like the same problem doesn't it?

The Good News is that somewhere tucked away in the character of God is the answer to every cry of the heart.

Below are listed some of God's character traits and attributes. Sometimes I like to read through the list while asking God to draw my attention to the one I need most in the moment. If He prompts you to do this, He will surely bless you. It is not enough to know about God. **We must know Him.**

He is our:

LOVE - 1 John 3:1	**JOY** – Psalms 4:7-8	**FATHER** – Galatians 4:4-7
FRIEND – James 2:23	**ROCK** – Psalms 62:1-8	**LIGHT** – 1 John 1:5-7
COUNSELOR – Psalms 119-:24	**MIRACLE WORKER** – John 20:30-31	**COMFORTER** – Matthew 5:4
SAVIOR – Matthew 1:21	**DELIVERER** – Psalms 34:1-7	**MERCY** - Titus 3:5-7
INTERCESSOR – 1Timothy 2:5	**WAY** – 1 Corinthians 10:13	**TRUTH** – John 8:31-32
LIFE – John 11:25-27	**VICTOR** – 1 Corinthians 15:51-57	**HOPE** – Hebrews 6:17-20

Some of His attributes are:

God is **Omniscient** – knowing all things

God is **Sovereign** – superior to all others, can do anything, and controls everything

God is **Omnipresent** – everywhere all the time

God is **Immutable** – unchangeable

God is **Omnipotent** – Almighty

God is **Supreme** – most high in authority, power and rank

God is **Faithful** – reliable, devoted, and dependable
God is **Wise** – always making right choices, keen perception
God is **Holy** – perfect in every way
God is **Eternal** – everlasting; without beginning or end
God is **Creator** – the One who brought the universe in to existence
God is **Good** – virtuous, upright, excellent, absolutely good
God is **Just** – impartial, correct, true, righteous

Lord, please come be our motivation to love. "If we love one another, God abides in us, and His love is perfected (matured) in us." 1 John 4:12 . I pray we denounce fear of punishment and embrace the love that casts out that fear. 1 John 4:18

Adoration/Praise: Hebrews 6:17-20
I praise You Lord. You are our HOPE. It is impossible for you to lie. We have strong encouragement . . . of the hope set before us.

Confession/Repentance: Matthew 1:21
I repent of trying to save myself when You have given me such a great grace.

Thanksgiving/gratitude: John 11:25-27, Psalm 111:10
Thank You God. Even when we die physically, we never die spiritually. We have eternity to learn and grow. Thank you that Your plan includes all who answer Your call and receive the gift You so freely give. With gratitude we receive Your lovingkindness and compassion.

Supplication/requests: GOD is WISE!
How foolish of us to lay claim to ourselves. (Galatians 3: 3) Please come and show us the way to combine our knowledge with reverential fear. Show us when we are being presumptuous or when we are being superstitious. We desperately need Your wisdom. Open our eyes to recognize You Lord as we walk through life and give us courage to cling to You, receive no deliverance except from You, and courage to proclaim, "I will not let You go until You bless me."

"Our own God shall bless us. God shall bless us." Psalm 67:6-7 KJV
AMEN

CHAPTER 10

MISCONCEPTIONS OF WHO GOD REALLY IS

MORE HINDERANCES TO FELLOWSHIP

We can all read the lists of His character traits and attributes. We can nod our heads in agreement and intellectually we know they are true. But in the recesses of our minds, on an emotional level, we just are not convinced. We are skeptical about God's true nature. The lists give us knowledge that must be tempered with awe and reverence.

Definition of reverence: Awareness that God is working through the people and events in my life to produce the character of Christ.

Charles Hadden Spurgeon said:

"Nothing happens to us that we would not wish for ourselves if we were as wise and loving as God."

It's no wonder we are perplexed by Spurgeon's statement. Our definition of wise and loving are limited to our human reasoning.

"For as the heavens are higher than the earth, so are His ways are higher than your ways, and His thoughts than your thoughts." Isaiah 55:9

As we read the list of God's <u>character</u> <u>traits</u> again with a renewed attitude of living an exchanged life that list takes on a whole new meaning.

We will never perfectly obtain the traits that set Him apart from everyone else, but our character will change for the better.

That is why it is important to examine a few of our misconceptions about God.

"There is a time to throw stones and a time to gather stones." Ec. 3:5

Remember the parable of the sower who sows the Word? Well, our misconceptions cause skepticism. Our skepticisms are like stones that hinder the word from taking firm root. And they are like fertilizer for the thorns that come up and cause us to yield no fruit of the Spirit.

The stones are there. We can discard them or use them to build barriers to fellowship. It is our choice; our terribly wonderful choice. If we chose to discard the stones and quit feeding the thorns that choke the Word, our God will honor our labors. To clear the land in order for the Sower to plant His precious seeds He invites us to enter into the process. Everything is under His control, but remember He hungers for fellowship with us. His timing and His order are always perfect.

He does the miraculous. We must do our part.
So, what is this labor He invites us to do? What is our part?
Prayer is the work. Prayer is our part!

But if you say, "Prayer is a mental exercise, not a way of life."

Listen – To – This

"It is the privilege of every Christian to live so fully in God that he never gets out of the *experienced* Presence for one moment. What before seemed mundane and non-spiritual now shines with a new light. A life lived in Christ becomes in a true sense a life of unceasing prayer: words are verbal prayers, deeds become prayers in action and even sleep may be but unconscious prayer. The whole mind may be placed so fully under the control of Christ that even sleep and forgetfulness work on our side to bless and help us in our practical waking lives." A.W. Tozer from <u>The Next Chapter After the Last</u>

What Tozer beautifully describes is the omnipresence of God. Holy Spirit is in us and in the world around us. "The heavens declare His righteousness, and all the peoples have seen His glory." Ps. 71:6

He goes before us and He has our back.

PRAYER IS OUR PRIVILEGE – A LABOR OF LOVE

For us to enter into the partnership that our honest seeking heart desires we must first relieve ourselves of the misconception that we are in a contract with God.

God's Offer of Salvation is an Unconditional Covenant

There is a vast difference between a contract and an unconditional covenant. Ours is a covenant relationship.

Contracts are common in our society. In our minds all our agreements are contingent on both parties holding up their end of the bargain.

Because we naturally filter everything we understand about God in terms of a contract we assume that if we don't abide by the terms of the agreement God will not hold up His end either. Because of this error in our thinking we find it nearly impossible to enter into the partnership that fulfills the desire of our hearts. His "experienced" presence eludes us.

No one must teach us this type of false "theology." We are born with a sense of what is fair and what is not fair. It doesn't seem fair to our soul (mind, will and emotions) that we do not have to do good works for God in order to stay in His good graces. But a branch detached from the Vine can only have fake fruit placed there by human hands. Just as a branch gets its life from the plant; we get our spiritual life from God. And then, some organized religions focus on our behavior and use the fear of punishment to try to keep everyone in line. Who would dare to approach a God Who is just waiting for us to screw up so that He can get even? The result is focusing on SELF. When we focus on SELF, guess what, SELF gets stronger not weaker.

Our God is approachable on the basis on the shed blood of Jesus Christ.
Instead of abiding by the terms of a contract,
God would have us abide in Him.

The truth is that God's unconditional covenant with us is based on His integrity. God sets the terms of the covenant and He makes the offer. Then we decide either to accept or reject His offer. Since Jesus has already satisfied and fulfilled our requirement, if we accept His offer, God is committed to treat us in light of our Savior's perfection even when we don't measure up.

There are consequences for maintaining our contract state of mind. We miss out on the joy of our salvation.

Have you ever tried to pull up or even trim a bush that has thorns? I have, and it makes you think twice about starting such a project. Religiosity wants us to think that sin is our problem and that we are supposed to do the work of the gardener. Gardens are not capable of pruning themselves. Our Heavenly Father prepares the soil, sows seeds and then lovingly prunes us so we can produce the fruit of His Spirit.

John 15: 1 "I am the true vine and My Father is the Vinedresser. Every branch in Me that does not bear fruit He takes away; and every branch that bears fruit, He prunes it, that it may bear more fruit."

If we avail ourselves of the indwelling Spirit, He will help us work out our salvation with reverence that produces awareness of God as He works through people and events in our lives. His heart's desire is to produce the character of Christ in us. As we partner with Him the result will be that we find ourselves convinced of His wisdom and His lovingkindness.

BACK TO WORK!

COVENANT PRAYER: TWO WAY COMMUNICATION

I dare say, most books that you read will not result in meeting the author or communicating in any way. How blessed are we, children of God, to be able to commune and communicate with the Author of the Bible and the Finisher of our faith! He is so sweet to speak to us today.

Living in His experienced presence is not a project to be completed or a program to the ignored. It is a process to be adored. We will never, this side of heaven, understand all His ways. But we will become like that which we give ourselves. If always trying to understand God's ways is our goal in life; the joy of embracing The Mystery will be lost.

Jesus is the Mystery of Godliness

In the New Testament a "Mystery" is not something that is impossible to understand. It is a plan or purpose of God that He has always known about but which He has withheld from the knowledge of humans until the time was right.

1 Timothy 3:16 KJV
"Without controversy great is the 'Mystery of Godliness,'
God was manifest (revealed) in the flesh,
Justified (vindicated) in the Spirit,
Beheld (seen) by angels,
Believed in the world, received up into glory."

The Mystery is that God revealed Himself by taking on human form and living among us. That is why Jesus could say, "He that hath seen Me hath seen the Father."

The Spirit's Indwelling Mankind

Another great "mystery" is that God withheld from men is the mystery of the "Divine Indwelling."

Col. 1:26-28 Paul calls it the mystery of "Christ in you," the hope of glory. When Jesus was received up into glory to be with the Father He said He would send the Spirit to **guide** us into all truth.

When we have a question as to His leading in a certain matter, we must wait for Him to speak.

We all must start somewhere, and I know I have acted presumptuously before and probably will again. Remember, presumption is taking our knowledge and proceeding without reverence. In reverence we will be willing to wait for God's direction and confirmation before we proceed on.

Knowledge must direct fear and fear must season knowledge.

It is much harder to hear His still small voice when we are stressed out and trying too hard.

There is a commonly known saying, "A bird in the hand is worth two in the bush."

That saying implies that we must try hard to hold on to what we have and look out for ourselves.

Our Lord says the very opposite is true.

He says, "I am Jehovah Jireh." I will provide – I will see to it.

As a child of God, I must hold "the bird" synonymous with any idea or blessing loosely with an open hand; not grasping anything. The Lord can give us exactly as many "birds" as we need.

For instance, I had no idea that the desire of my heart was to write a book. When the time was right the desire emerged.

Two or three times in the last year a thought came to my mind. The thought was, "I don't know how anyone can write a book; all those words and pages of words, I don't have a book in me."

That was God's way of introducing me to the idea of myself as an author and His way of establishing me as insufficient to the task. He is the All Sufficient One.

Another thought that propelled me on down the path was this:

Swimmers swim – Bikers bike – Writers write

This was like a wakeup call. I began to envision myself as a writer. An idea I could not have conceived of a year ago now seemed possible.

There is no need to go on a treasure hunt trying to find a new project. His call will come when He knows we are ready. Then we can rest in His loving arms. He is at work in our world and He invites us to enter in.

In this life we are given many NOW words; as Gary Wilkerson put it. Some "now" words come as a blessed relief and some come with conviction and correction. If our disposition (attitude about life) is one of submission, we will pray something like this:

I believe You gave me this idea. I will lay it at the foot of the
cross and trust that You will do what You do best; lead me
and make it possible for me to fulfill this desire.

Lord, help us not become obsessed with an idea. The true object of our desire is You, Lord Jesus. You are the Word. So, I will <u>not</u> hold this "bird" near and dear. I will let this idea rest on my hand and trust that You are my COUNSELOR. Instead of holding on to an idea we will hold on to You. And we will not let You go until You bless us. Amen

"Delight yourself in the Lord and He will give you the desires of your heart." Psalm 37 4

Desire defined: (noun) appetite. Craving for something in particular; something of Gods choosing.

If an idea is conceived in the heart of God and born in the heart of man we can proclaim, "Thank You Lord for the desire You have placed in my heart!"

He entrusts a desire to us, but we must trust Him to confirm Himself by working out details that bring about the original desire.

Entrust defined: To put something into someone's care and protection

We Trust God – He Entrusts Us With Desires

I am belaboring this point because I have been mistaken before about the origination of a desire.

One of the best examples of a misplaced desire is an incident that happened in the life of a married couple we know. They had put their house up for sale. Another very nice couple looked at the house and then returned to say that the Lord told them that the house was for them and then they said the exact amount God had told them to pay. That price was thousands below the selling price. Our friends, who also knew the Lord, said that they did not hear God say that they should lower their asking price. This transaction did not take place, but someone did come along shortly who paid the fair market value of the house.

I don't recount this incident to pass judgement on anyone. It serves as a warning that ideas conceived in our minds may not come to pass. If they really could not afford the house, they were better off not purchasing it. A bird in the hand could prove to be more than we can handle. It would be better if it flew away. Our Lord does want to partner with us, but God forbid we name Him as a "credible partner" in order to get what we want.

Answered Prayer
by an Unknown Confederate Soldier

I asked God for strength, that I might achieve,
I was made weak, that I might learn humbly to obey . . .
I asked for health, that I might do greater things,
I was given infirmity, that I might do better things . . .

I asked for riches, that I might be happy, I was
given poverty that I might be wise . . .
I asked for power, that I might have the praise of men,
I was given weakness, that I might feel the need of God . . .
I asked for all things, that I might enjoy life,
I was given life, that I might enjoy all things . . .
I got nothing that I asked for but everything I had hoped for;
almost despite myself, my unspoken prayers were answered,
I am among all men most richly blessed.

The soldier who wrote these words most certainly had learned to lay his ideas at the foot of the cross and trust that God knew what was best. As he lived the exchanged life the true desires of his heart, that had been there all along, were revealed.

His <u>Father,</u> Who <u>knows all things,</u> <u>delivered</u> him from his ways and showed him the everlasting <u>Way</u>. <u>The Truth</u> set him free, <u>worked miracles</u> in his life and gave him <u>hope</u>. The <u>joy</u> of the Lord was his strength and gratitude became a mainstay of his life.

Surely <u>Goodness</u> and <u>Mercy</u> followed him all the days of his life
and he will dwell in the house of the <u>Lord</u> forever. (Paraphrase Ps. 23:6)

Could it be that when we don't get what we really want we probably get something we really need?

When God speaks words of power to our spirit it is very personal. The word comes with power to set us free to grow where we are planted. It is in the process that we learn to know the true desires of our heart; the desires He has always had for us. When we reason with Him, we find ourselves receiving the exact "word" we need in the moment. Our hearts exchange and the partnership grows. The little I am grows weaker and The Great I Am becomes dominate. It's a little like ballroom dancing. One must lead while the other one follows but the partnership becomes so natural that a casual observer would not see the subtle nudges and slight movements that the leader imparts. The two appear to be moving as one. Jesus asked the Father that He not take us out of the world but that we would be one with Him as He and the Father are One. John 10:30, John 17: 15,21a

GUIDANCE
author unknown

Dancing with God When I meditated on the word Guidance, I kept seeing "dance" at the end of the word.

I remember reading that doing God's will is a lot like dancing. When two people try to lead,
nothing feels right . . .
The movement doesn't flow with the music, and everything is quite uncomfortable and jerky.
When one realizes that, and lets the other lead, both bodies begin to flow with the music.
One gives gentle cues, perhaps with a nudge to the back or by pressing lightly in one direction or another.
It's as if two become one body, moving beautifully. The dance takes surrender, willingness and attentiveness from one person and guidance and skill from the other.
My eyes drew back to the word Guidance. When I saw "G": I thought of God, followed by "u" and "I".

"God, "u" and "I" dance."

As I lowered my head, I became willing to trust that I would get guidance about my life.
Once again, I became willing to let God lead. My prayer for you today is that God's blessings and mercies are upon you on this day and every day.

My prayer for the reader of this book – May you abide in God, as God abides in you. Dance together with God, trusting God to lead and guide you through each season of your life. Amen

WALTZ THROUGH LIFE?

Wouldn't it be wonderful if we could waltz through life without a care from the moment we accept Jesus as our Savior? Our problem is our flesh that must be trained to obey the Word of God.

About ten years ago Mike and I took dance lessons. We had no idea what we were getting ourselves into. The instructor started out showing us the correct steps for a particular dance and then insisted that we look up into the face of our partner when everything in us wanted to look down at our own feet. Then there was the rhythm of the music and the swirl of activity when other couples were dancing nearby. Each time we seemed to master a basic level the instructor pressed us on deeper into the technique required to advance on. About the time we felt a little comfortable with our progress there was a time of practice, practice, and more practice before starting over with a different dance style; then the process was repeated. There were times when the learning was so frustrating we wanted to give up and times of enjoying it immensely. We met wonderful people at the dance studio, and it opened up a social life we had no idea existed.

It took years for me to see the parallel between dancing and our relationship with God, but it was there all along.

When we first accept Christ's invitation, we realize the Bible is our textbook. But it takes time to see the Holy Spirit as our instructor. At first, we look to ourselves to fulfill what we see as our obligations, but everything seems out of rhythm. The peace and joy of the Lord eludes us. Even when things seem to be moving nicely the Instructor bids us go deeper and lower.

He says, "Practice My Presence - Practice My Presence - Practice My Presence."

I can't overstate the frustration of trying to dance when it is as foreign to you as learning to speak a new language. After a while you develop what is called "muscle memory" and the process flows nicely. Without the problems of life, we would never get in God's rhythm or recognize His divine order.

The dance of life takes surrender, willingness and attentiveness from us and guidance from the God who indwells us.

"All discipline for the moment seems not to be joyful, but sorrowful; yet to those who have been trained by it, afterwards it yields the peaceful fruit of righteousness. "Hebrews 12:11

Getting Into God's Stride

"Getting into God's stride means nothing less than union with Himself. It takes a long time to get there but keep at it. Don't give in because the pain is bad just now, get on with it, and before long you will find you have a new vision and a new purpose." Oswald Chambers <u>My Utmost for His Highest</u>

Partner defined: (noun) A person who takes part in an undertaking with another or others.

In 1 John 1:5-7 , John describes the fullest possible partnership, fellowship and union with God and others.

"And this is the message we have heard from Him and announce to you,
that God is light, and in Him that is no darkness at all
If we say that we have fellowship with Him and yet walk in the darkness,
we lie and do not practice the truth.
But if we walk in the light as He Himself is in the light,
we have fellowship with one another,
and the blood of Jesus His Son cleanses us from all sin."

CHAPTER 11

OUR STUBBORN
SELF WILL

ANOTHER HUNDERANCE TO FELLOWSHIP

If surrender and willingness to follow God are necessary for fellowship, then our stubborn self-will is necessary for us to maintain control.

Stubbornness defined: A trait found in persons who are only willing to change when outward circumstances force them to.

There are problems and tragedies that come our way in this life that we do not bring on ourselves. They are not the result of our attitudes or actions. But some of the circumstances that surround us are the direct result of our being self-centered.

When we look at the creation of man, we see God's design for His Son. He was selfless in His desire and design. We were made in God's image and only being God-centered will satisfy our deepest longing. Man was made to give himself to God and become a blessing.

What is needed are many exchanges of heart. When we have reached our wit's end the Holy Spirit is waiting with open arms to receive us.

The Parable of the Two Prodigals - Luke 15:11-32

The parable traditionally called the parable of the Prodigal Son is an example of our human self-will set against Father God, and the Father God's desire to welcome us home.

The word prodigal has more than one meaning.

Prodigal defined:

(1) exceedingly or recklessly wasteful with money
(2) extremely generous; lavish

The two definitions are in stark contrast. The first one is self-serving. The other is descriptive of the father in the parable who was extremely generous.

From this we see that the father in the parable was prodigal also. We have heard the word used in a negative connotation for so long it feels wrong to think of the father as a prodigal. Nevertheless, it is true.

I think Jesus used this illustration to give us insight into human nature and Father God's nature also. According to the terms of the covenant His generosity is unparalleled and absolute.

Let's examine the text; verses 11-24

Jesus said, "A certain man had two sons."

The younger of the two asked his father to give him his share of the family estate.

At the request of the younger son the father divided the family wealth between his two sons. According to Deut. 21:17 the first born received a double portion of the wealth.

A few days later the younger son went on a journey to a distant country and when he was there, he squandered his part of the money on loose living.

He wanted independence from the father and independence is what he got for himself.

It is safe to say that Jesus' use of the term "loose living" was an indictment of his behavior. In Luke 16:11 Jesus said, "If therefore you have not been faithful in the use of unrighteous mammon who will entrust true riches to you?" True riches being spiritual responsibilities.

The son's self-indulgent extravagant lifestyle caught up with him. When he had spent everything, a severe famine occurred in the country to which he had gone; and he found himself in great need.

He got a job feeding swine. For a Jewish man it was the lowest most humiliating job he could have taken. He was starving and wanting to fill his stomach with the food that the swine were eating. He had spread his wealth around but now no one would give him so much as a farthing. When He came to his senses, he said to himself, "How many of my father's men have more than enough bread, but I am dying here with hunger!" I will get up and go to my father and will say to him, "Father I have sinned against heaven and your sight; I am no longer worthy to be called your son; make me as one of your hired men."

Our most basic need is for love and acceptance.

In our fleshly self-centered way, we seem bent on trying to pacify those needs with our idols.

Look at it this way. If a very young child was only given a pacifier he would starve to death. That's what we do when we exclude God and pacify our need/longing for love and acceptance with things other than God.

Spiritually we starve to death.

But like the younger son we seem to have to go to some lengths before we realize that maintaining control of our lives is not the answer.

"You don't know that Jesus is all you need until Jesus is all you've got." Michael Wells

Our God is a jealous God, but he will not force our surrender and willingness to follow Him. He is patient and ready to deliver us when we cry out "Hosanna, save me. Rescue me!"

What are we saved from?

We are saved from hell for eternity and we are saved from our selves this side of heaven. The far country will always impoverish us and starve us spiritually.

Before the younger son could deliver his rehearsed speech, his father saw him coming, felt compassion for him, ran to hug him and kissed him.

> "Love is patient, love is kind, and is not jealous;
>   love does not brag and is not arrogant,
> Does not act unbecomingly; it does not seek its own
>   is not provoked, does not take into account

a wrong suffered, does not rejoice in
unrighteousness, but rejoices with truth."
"Love bears all things, believes all things, hopes all things,
endures all things. Love never fails. 1 Corinthians 13:4-8a

The words of Godly love stored up in the fathers' heart flowed from his mouth.

He did not take opportunity to rebuke this son that was dead in his spirit and lost in his soul.

Jesus said of Himself, "The Son of man has come to save that which was lost (damaged, decimated and perishing)." Matt. 18:11 The father could have crushed him with angry words, but he didn't have it in Him to criticize. As the parable goes on, he told the slaves to hurry and bring out the best robe and put it on him and put a ring on his hand and sandals on his feet. Then he declared a celebration. He said, "Let us eat and rejoice because this son of mine that was dead has come to life again. He was lost and has been found."

The younger son had loved the darkness.

He had danced with the Devil and lived to tell about it.

Acknowledgment of his sin had begun the
process of reconciliation with his father.

**There is a way through our darkest night if
we humble ourselves as a child.**

Matthew 18:2-5 Jesus said, "Truly I say to you, unless you are converted and become like children, you shall not enter in the kingdom of heaven."

Children are open to new ideas, exhibit a trusting nature and are willing to learn. These childlike qualities constitute the fertile soil that allows His beloved seeds to grow.

Jesus requested that the Father not ". . . take us out of this dark world but to keep us from the evil one." (John 17:15) "We are called out of darkness into His marvelous light." (1 Peter 2:9) He knows that without the darkness we would never let the "Morning star arise in our hearts". (2 Peter 1:19)

"God is light, and in Him there is no darkness at all. If we say that we have fellowship with Him and yet walk in the darkness we lie and do not practice the truth; but if we walk in the light as He Himself is in the light, we have fellowship with one another, and the blood of Jesus His Son cleanses us from all sin." 1 John 5:6-7

Fellowship defined: Fellowship is the love which fills the hearts of believers for one another and for God.

God is the source of all light – physical, intellectual and spiritual.

For many years the procedure for developing photographs required a time in darkness. It was the job of the developer to take the negative and through a series of tasks, including a chemical bath, use the negative image to produce the positive. As a result of the process a picture gradually emerged. The "positive" was there all along but we could not see it.

That process is a lot like our lives.

I have found God's dealing with me to be similar to that dark room. When I come to the end of myself; the exact realization I need is available to me. His character has been developed in me in spite of myself. When dwelling in His presence, He will bring light to the hidden things when we are ready to let go of them. I cannot clean myself up for Him. That's His job and He is very good at it.

If we are truly converted, "God causes all things to work together for our good to those who love God, to those who are called according to His purpose." (Romans 8:28) If we have not allowed Christ to be our savior then the dark room is all we will ever know. It has been said that for those who harden their hearts and refuse the light – this world is the only "heaven" they will ever experience; how sad and how unnecessary.

John 3:19 "And this is the judgement, that the light is come into the world, and men loved the darkness rather than the light; for their deeds where evil."

John 3:20 "He who practices the truth comes to the light, that his deeds may be wrought (fashioned, molded, created) in God." (explanation mine)

Christians that practice His presence, as a way of everyday life, will find themselves drawn to the Light like a moth to a flame. In the process, only the deeds done in the flesh will burn away leaving us with deeds fashioned, molded and created by God.

In the book of Daniel, chapter 3, Shadrach, Meshach and Abednego refused to bow to the golden image that King Nebuchadnezzar had set out on the plain and commanded the people to worship. They joined the chorus of saints who have said, "If I perish, I perish." As a result, they were thrown into the fiery furnace, but they were not consumed. Only the ropes that bound them were burned as they themselves walked freely within the fire.

Even King Nebuchadnezzar had to admit that, "There is no god who is able to deliver in this way." vs.29d

> He also said – "How great are His signs, and
> how mighty are His wonders!
> His kingdom is an everlasting Kingdom, and His
> dominion is from generation to generation."
> Daniel 4:3

It has been said, "It takes a greater pleasure to replace a lesser pleasure."

There is no greater pleasure than to draw from the well of living water, drink some and pass it on to others.

Our goal as believers is not to love the darkness. We are to be in the world but not of the world. The more we submit to God in the midst of darkness the more the image of God is visible. These momentary afflictions will produce the blessed reward of His love _experienced_ and _expressed_ in our life. We are called to be light. We are not called to condemn the world but to be a contrast; a positive influence in a negative world.

Experienced defined: an activity that includes training, observation, practice and personal participation, knowledge and skill resulting from the partnership

Expressed defined: an action flowing from one's inner being the source of which is God Himself

The younger son is a perfect example of how Luke 14:11 and Matt. 23:11-12 complement each other.

"Everyone who exalts himself shall be humbled and everyone who humbles himself shall be exalted." Luke 14:11

"The greatest among you (those exalted ones)
will be your servant." Matt. 23; 11-12

After his ordeal the prodigal son was ready to be a servant.

His name had been Selfish Prodigal.

Now, God has changed his name to Selfless Servant.

He was willing to be a servant <u>only</u>, but the father would not let that request stand. He welcomed him back as a son willing to serve. The father's behavior displayed his generous spirit.

The younger brother had been one of the "younger generation". Now he has had his own Red Sea experience. Now he has seen the outstretched arm of love, acceptance and protection the Father offers to all His children.

Our life experiences can serve us well if we realize that there are many more bearers to fellowship to be dealt with in God's time and in God's way.

Gratitude often comes just before an exchange of heart.

The son's lack of contentment mirrors our own. And it propelled him to go on a journey looking for the love and acceptance he already had.

The younger son had lavishly spent his wealth. Other people no doubt prospered, but the root of pleasure seeking produced the fruit of sin.

Generosity can be Godly, or it can be used to
selfishly live out the fantasy our imaginations came up with.
But in the end, we will come up against Reality and
either rightly relate to the Father through the Son
or
we will relate to other humans who will
gladly encourage flesh to flourish.

Of course, it comes easy to the natural man to relate to other humans. It takes a supernatural work of the Holy Spirit to bring us into relation with Almighty God.

This personal inner turmoil is not to be avoided at all cost. If we submit to Him, God will use that churning to propel us on down the well-worn narrow path that leads to the near country called, "God In You the Hope of Glory."

Paul said, "I have learned to be content in whatever circumstance I am." Philippians 4:11 . Whether Paul had a little or a lot he found his contentment in Christ. He said, "I can do all things through Him who strengthens me." Philippians 4:13

There is a vast difference between being content and just settling for a nominal Christian life of following a list of rules.

Paul also said, "I do not regard myself as having laid hold of it yet; but this one thing I do: forgetting what lies behind and reaching forward to what lies ahead, I press on toward the goal for the prize of the upward call of God in Christ Jesus." Philippians 3:13-14

We mistake wanting more and more of what this world has to offer with wanting more of what heaven has in store for us. Our old nature wants heaven on earth.

Matthew 6: 19-20 "Do not lay up for yourselves treasures upon earth, where moth and rust destroy, and where thieves break in and steal. But lay up for yourselves treasures in heaven, where neither moth nor rust destroys, and where thieves do not break in and steal."

The indwelling of the Spirit of God is a foretaste of what our life will be like then.'

The Bible says that when we see Him, we will be like Him.

"Beloved now we are children of God, and it has not appeared as yet what we shall be. We know that, when He appears, we shall be like Him, because we shall see Him just as He is." 1 John 3:2

In 1 Thessalonians 4: 16-17 Paul says; "For the Lord Himself will descend from heaven with a shout, with the voice of the archangel, and with the trumpet of God; and the dead in Christ shall rise first. Then we who are alive and remain shall be caught up together with them in the clouds to meet the Lord in the air, and thus we shall always be with the Lord."

Compared to eternity, this life *is a momentary light affliction* that is producing for us a crown of glory. He is using this life to prepare us for life eternal.

I believe the universe is young and that in the age to come there are many adventures and ecstasies awaiting those who have died to self and risen from the deathbed called self-sufficiency.

God uses our fear of physical death or eternal separation from God to press us into choosing this day whom we will serve. Will we serve ourselves or God?

We expect Satan to attack us in the areas where our character is weak, but he knows that our strengths, under his influence, can be our undoing.

People like the younger brother probably have a generous nature. But I have come to believe that our giftings from God are a bullseye target to the enemy of our souls. If he can tempt and convince us to take a positive, God-given, trait and submit it to Satan; then he has a foothold in our lives.

"For our struggle is not against flesh and blood but against the rulers, against the powers, against the world forces of this darkness, against the spiritual forces of wickedness in the heavenly places." Ephesians 6:12

If you tend to be a tenderhearted person, Satan will drive you to distraction hurting for others. If he can confuse tender hearted compassion for self-centered indulgence, he has you right where he wants you. But that is not the end of the story. As God allows Satan to assault us with his carnal/fleshly weapons we begin to "get real" with God and learn that the weapons of our warfare are not carnal or fleshly. Our weapons are spiritual, and Satan is no match for Lord God Almighty.

The answer to every problem of mankind is tucked away somewhere in the character of God!

HE IS OUR DELIVERER!

When temptation comes along the line of our tendency to sin the Lord uses it as a reminder of just how much we need Him. At that time gratitude for past, present, and future deliverance brings us right back from the brink of another trip to the far country. It is as simple as an honest prayer. He said, "Ask, seek and knock" . . . exactly what you need will be given to you, things lost will be found and mysteries of the Kingdom will be opened to you. (Matthew 7:7-8 my paraphrase) Now the stronghold that the enemy has erected has been taken over by our Lord and <u>freedom</u> is ours. Christ is Lord of our lives!

**Gratitude is the key that unlocks the door
to our self-imposed prison.**

**WHEN WE ARE WEAK IN THE FLESH,
WE ARE STRONG IN THE LORD!**

Let's go back and finish examining the text. Luke 15:28-30

The Older Brother's Reaction

In his own way, the older brother loved the darkness. He embraced rules of behavior, saw himself as successful, and not in need of redemption.

In the last book of the bible, John spoke these words of warning to the church At Laodicea:

> "So because you are lukewarm, and neither hot nor cold,
> I will spit you out of My mouth. Because you say, I am
> rich, and have become wealthy, and have need of nothing,
> and you do not know that you are wretched and miserable
> and poor and blind and naked." Revelation 3:16-17

Luke 15: 28-30 "He (the older brother) became angry, and was not willing to go into the party for his brother. His father came out and began entreating him. The older brother said to his father. 'Look, for so many years I have been serving you, and have never neglected a command of yours; and yet you have never given me a kid (not even a measly goat!) that I might be merry with my friends." (explanation mine)

Then he proceeded to grumble about the fatted calf the younger brother had received even though his brother's behavior had been so subpar. The older brothers' self-righteous comments and lack of compassion revealed the true condition of his heart. He, like most of us, gain comfort from our self-righteous habit of comparing ourselves to others. His name could have changed to "One Not Worthy to Judge Another" but his name did NOT change.

Matthew said, "Judge not lest you be judged. For in the way you judge, you will be judged; by your standard of measure it will be measured to you." Matthew 7:1-2

We have all been there. We've all been sure that our evaluation of a situation was flawless. When we speak words that cause others to see our self-righteousness; our judgmental attitude comes back on our heads. The above text is proven true.

Isn't it just like us to honor our contract frame of mind more than the Heavenly Father's covenant love? We grumble and complain wanting more and more when we are in His debt and only the precious blood of Jesus will satisfy One so Holy.

The older brother represents the human condition focused on "good" behavior. He had **not** come to the realization that self, behaving well apart from God, is the same as drawing water from the well called self-sufficiency. It will never satisfy God's requirement of holiness. He needed the spiritual water that Jesus offered the Samaritan women. No wonder Jesus portrayed him as lacking love for his brother. In his contract state of mind, he didn't think he was in need of forgiveness.

On an emotional level God's covenant love seems too good to be true.

It has been said, "Emotions are the best of servants and the worst of masters." Kathy Freeburg

Eugen Peterson explains God's love this way:

"God gets down on His knees among us; gets on our level and shares Himself with us. He does not reside afar off and send diplomatic messages, He kneels among us . . . God shares Himself generously and graciously."

God said that He would never leave us or forsake us. If there is distance between us it is because we have chosen to go on a journey and pretend He decided to stay home.

He shares Himself in the exact way He chooses and when He knows we are ready to move on down the road with Him. He created us and He knows that our human strengths easily become our vulnerabilities. The choice is ours to make. Will we submit ourselves to the Lord who gets down on His knees among us? Will we give Him creative control?

Sometimes we find ourselves feeling as worthless as the younger son or as full of false worth as the older son.

Remember, our feelings and our emotions about God's character can be a hindrance to experiencing His full blessing. Neither are our feelings about ourselves an accurate measure of our worth to God.

When the prodigal son realized his helplessness, God gave him hope for a bright tomorrow and a chance to live well the life he had been given.

HIDDEN BEAUTY AND A LIFE WELL LIVED

In this world there are many kinds of wood for various purposes.
And then there is the natural wood that drifts on
bodies of water and eventually washes ashore.
It appears to be totally worthless. But in reality,
it was formed by the Creator.
Its purpose hidden from the human eye.
The Creator has craftsmen; artists who see potential
and set out to reveal that beautiful purpose.
They will be as gentle as possible as they remove
the debris, dirt and rotten wood.
They take a worthless piece of wood and transform it into a work of art.
As I ponder that truth, I can't help but think of people
who feel abandoned, lost and worthless.
The difference in this analogy is that the wood has no choice – we do!
The Creator-Craftsman has not given up. He will
be as gentle as possible as He removes
old baggage; damaged emotions and self-destructive behavior patterns;
gradually revealing a beautiful image of Himself.
Jesus asked the cripple man at the pool of
Bethesda "Do you want to be healed?"
Then He said, "Take up your bed and walk." John 5:6, 8

God does the miraculous. We must do our part.
The process may seem painful for a time, but
sorrow and joy make up a life well lived.

Jesus said, "Apart from Me you can do nothing." John 15:5

"I can do all things through Jesus Christ who
strengthens me." Philippians 4:13

**Jeremiah spoke words to encourage his
people in a time of great sorrow.**

He spoke God's words to the Jews who were living in exile in Babylon because of their rebellion. They were literally living in a far country. Praise God, these words still have relevance for us today.

"For I know the plans I have for you, declares the Lord, plans for welfare and not for calamity to give you a future and a hope. Then you will call upon Me and come and pray to Me, and I will listen to you, and you will seek Me and find Me, when you seek Me with all your heart." Jeremiah 29:11-13

THE PARABLE CONCLUDES

The father has a final word for the older son. He said to him, "My child, you have always been with me, and all that is mine is yours." (vs. 31)

Could it be that Jesus is trying to communicate to us that ingratitude is a portable prison we take with us everywhere we go?

In the final verse the father appeals to his emotion and his sense of compassion. He reminds him that the prodigal son is his brother.

"But we had to be merry and rejoice, for this **brother of yours** was dead and has begun to live, and was lost and has been found." (Emphasis mine) (Verse 32)

A BLESSED TRUTH:

God goes with us on our journey. He is right there preparing us for the true spiritual riches and responsibilities to come.

He makes it possible for us to learn to respond – to – His – ability.

Dearest Father God, thank you for loving us even when we are at our worst. Thank you, Holy Spirit, for showing us who we really are. Thank You for the comfort that comes from knowing we are not alone. Thank you, Jesus, Miracle of the ages, for the deliberate act of Your will to lay down Your life for we ungrateful human beings.

> Whether we spend our life on "bad behavior"
> or on supposed "good behavior";
> when we have spent it all, then and only then,
> will we realize that we are bankrupt
> of spirit and reach out to You for healing.

Thank You Jesus. You made it possible for us to drink the Spiritual water and find refreshment for our souls. You said there was more hope for sinners (those whose sin is obvious) than for the Pharisees whose sin was hidden behind a pretense of righteousness; both have a heart that needs exchanging. You did not say there was no hope for the latter ones. It may just take a different kind of dark room to reveal their true identity. Thank you, God Almighty, for redeeming our wanderings, using the valuable lessons we learn, and giving your blessed Hope to every honest seeking heart. AMEN

"I TELL YOU THERE IS JOY IN THE PRESENCE OF THE
ANGELS OF GOD OVER ONE SINNER WHO REPENTS."
Luke 15:10

CHAPTER 12

OUR GOD IS TRIUNE, THE GREAT THREE IN ONE

Father - Son – Holy Spirit

We are created in His image and have three parts
to our being: body, soul and spirit.

The five senses of the body are sight, hearing, smell, taste, and touch.

THESE FIVE SENSES MAKE UP THE FLESH OF MANKIND.

Our body is the outer part that presents itself to the world. The five senses of the body give us opportunity for the body to convey information to the soul (mind, will and emotions). The mind takes the information from the senses and then it uses it to explore the world, analyze stimuli, communicate with other people and for self-expression. The self that's expressed is either under the control of the natural man or the indwelling Spirit of God.

SIGHT AND HEARING

The senses of sight and hearing stimulate the imagination. As any artist knows imagination is the spark that ignites creativity. But for the person locked in a self-imposed prison of fear, imagination can ignite the "what if" syndrome or "sin"drome as it has been called. Curiosity and impatience to know the future fuels that very dangerous fire. This kind of imagination – run - wild can propel the soul to seek the counsel of the underworld. Or by contrast, imagination can be a blessed relief when it releases creativity into the world and is a blessing to everyone fortunate enough to experience it.

Creativity defined:

> "Creativity is a kind of passion that takes
> something God has already made,
> forms it in a way that is new to us and pleasing
> to the senses." (author unknown)

Our relationship with God is on a need – to - know basis with Him in charge. There are many things that we are better off not seeing, hearing or knowing.

Proverbs 25:2 "It is the glory of God to conceal a thing."

Oswald Chambers put it this way: "Men will not wait for the slow, steady majestic way of God; they try to enter in by this door and that door. The barriers are placed by a Holy God, and He has told us clearly – "Not that way." God grant we may accept His clouds and mysteries and be led into His inner secrets by obedient trust."

HEARING

The mind is amazing in its ability to remember what it hears. Spoken words have power to influence people around us. If an adult tells a child that he is a genius; life will either confirm that as true or prove it untrue. Our pre-conceptions of ourselves are usually not rooted or grounded in complete truth. It is the project of a lifetime to discover who we really are. God knows us and remember He gave us weaknesses to shatter our self-sufficiency and problems to display His provisions. His slow majestic way tests our resolve to seek no deliverance except from Him.

The reward for perseverance is the gift of hearing our Lords voice. He speaks to us through His written word and His still small voice He speaks to our heart. He speaks words of life and light and joy even in our darkest hour.

"Faith comes from hearing, and hearing by the word of Christ." Romans 10:17

SMELL

Another of the five senses is smell. It corresponds with the soul's conscience. It is our conscience that makes us uncomfortable when our attitudes and actions are wrong. It also can be the place in our mind that discerns good and evil. At some time in our lives most of us have used the phrase, "That smells fishy." It means that you are not sure, but something just does not seem right.

When the human spirit is illumined by the Holy Spirit, we call it discernment. Discernment is a blessed gift from God to show us truth about our behavior. Our conscience is not always an accurate assessment. It can be deceived, or it can be used by God to convict us of our sins. Repentance is a key element of our relationship with Him.

When the human soul is **not** aligned with Gods Spirit, we live out of the tree of the Knowledge of Good and Evil. Always searching for "facts" but never coming to the Truth. In our soulish way, we are wise in our own eyes.

Isaiah 5:20-21 "Woe to those who call evil good and good evil; who substitute darkness for light and light for darkness . . . Woe to those who are wise in their own eyes."

Would be better to allow our minds to be trained by God's written word and to go to Him in prayer trusting Him to be the Wise One. He will illumine our path, give us wisdom and show us how to rightly represent Him to the world.

2 Corinthians 2:14-16 But thanks be to the God who always leads us in His Triumph in Christ and manifests through us the sweet aroma of the knowledge of Him in every place. For we are a fragrance of Christ to God among those who are being

saved and among those who are perishing; to the one an aroma from death to death, to the other an aroma from life to life.

TASTE

As the body tastes food, it compares flavors and decides its' likes and dislikes. The person who is relinquishing control of self to God will observe contrasts, compare facts and if they search wide enough and deep enough, they will find the truth behind all the hype the world has to offer.

Jesus said, "I am the Bread of Life" and David said, "Oh taste and see that the Lord is good." Psalm 34:8

TOUCH

The spirit does receive stimuli of outward and natural things through the soul and body. The body's sense of touch corresponds with the human spirits sense of affection. When we are separated from someone we love the longing to touch and be touched grows with each passing day.

Oh, that we children of God longed for His touch.

Since Jesus is not physically here on earth those of us that love Him make up the living organism capable of being touched by Him and touching the world for Christ.

In this age we live in, His touch is <u>experienced</u> through the gifts of faith, hope, worship, prayer and an unexplainable love for God and mankind. His love is <u>expressed</u> through the ministries of God that are spread abroad by His Spirit and through His children.

Among the ministries of the Spirit of God are guiding, teaching, assuring and praying.

Jesus said the Spirit will <u>guide</u> and <u>teach</u> us. "But when He, the Spirit of truth comes, He will guide you into all truth." John 16:13

Paul says that the Spirit will <u>assure</u> us that we are children of God. "The Spirit Himself bears witness with our spirit that we are children of God, and if children, heirs also, heirs of God and fellow heirs with Christ, if indeed we suffer with Him in order that we may also be glorified with Him." Romans 8:16

The Spirit prays for us. "The Spirit helps our weakness; for we do not know how to pray as we should but the Spirit Himself intercedes for us with groanings too deep for words." Romans 8:26

Paul also said ". . . pray at all times in the Spirit, and with this in view, be on the alert with all perseverance and petition for all the saints." Ephesians 6:18

"The fruit of the Spirit is love, joy, peace, patience, kindness, goodness, faithfulness, gentleness, self-control; against such things there is no law." Galatians 5:22

Out of these fruits will come opportunities to teach and guide each other. We will find ourselves assuring others. We will pray for them and we will be prayed for by them.

It is as though we say to each other, "Lets lock arms and walk out this life together."

"My hope is from Him." Psalm 62:5

"We exult in our tribulations, knowing that tribulation brings about perseverance; and perseverance, proven character; and proven character, hope; and hope does not disappoint, because the love of God has been poured out within our hearts through the Holy Spirit who was given to us." Romans 5:3-5

Because of His indwelling Spirit we can rise to every occasion.

"Just as the body without the spirit is dead, so also faith without works is dead." James 2:26

My paraphrase – Living faith will display His abilities.

Works done out of our self-sufficiency produce dead works. Dead works have nothing of the supernatural about them. There is no vision from God. Others do not smell the aroma of God or taste that He is good. His touch is absent.

LAST BUT NOT LEAST

The Whole-Body Sensory Connection

I would like to introduce you to a physical sense that is little talked about. A sense that I believe parallels with the human "spirit."

We are keenly aware of our five senses of sight, hearing, smell, taste and touch. But there is a little-known sense that functions without our being consciously self-aware of it. It is the fascia or connective tissue that is found everywhere in the body. It is a casing that interpenetrates and surrounds all organs and holds every, bone, blood vessel, muscle and organ in its proper place.

The "fascia" is made up of elastin, collagen and fibers that are awash in cellular fluid. This fluid allows oxygen, nutrients and waste to move from cell to cell. In order for the fascia to do its job it must be adequately hydrated. When it is hydrated, we are able to respond to the world around us in a marvelous way.

Have you ever wondered how we are able to talk and walk at the same time? It has been widely accepted that the brain is in charge of all muscle and joint movement. But, unless the person is disabled, we do not have to think about walking; we just do it. The connective tissue sends a huge amount of information to the brain and the whole body. Our bodies constantly use this information.

I love the fact that the fascia seems hidden. We can't point to it like the eyes, ears, nose, tongue, or skin but it receives information from outside and inside the body. Its impact on our everyday life is profound as our bodies constantly regulate joint position and stability.

The spirit of man has intelligence;
It is persuasive and influences our actions in
a subtle almost imperceptible way.
The Christian spirit is constantly influencing and
persuading us to love God and honor Him.
It is our soul that seeks its own salvation.
Just as we can use all our senses for good or evil so can the
soul be directed to obey God's voice or ignore Him.
The soul is made up of the mind, will intellect and emotions.
It is the soul of mankind that passes worldly information to the spirit.
The human heart, soul and spirit are in desperate
need of the salvation that Jesus offers.
The heart is deceitful above all things, and desperately
sick, who can know it? Jeremiah 17:9

In Psalm 51 verse 19 David made a request of God. He said, Create
in me a clean heart, O God, and renew a right spirit within me.
The physical heart takes action and pumps blood to every part of
the body so does the spiritual heart drive the will toward action.
Let's go back and review what is necessary for the
physical connective tissue to work properly.
It must be well oxygenated and hydrated; it must receive
nutrients and waste materials must be able to be released.
Now let's examine this analogy to see if the
parallels hold any insights for us.

OXYGEN

Humans can live without food for weeks and without water for days,
but we can only live minutes without oxygen. From the first breathe we
take until our last, the need never diminishes; neither do we ever reach a
place where we need less of God. In fact, the more we grow in God the
more we recognize our need of Him.

The oxygen our cells require comes from the air we breathe. Cellular
respiration is the process by which the cells use oxygen to break down
sugar; producing the energy that our bodies need.

The Spirit is spoken of as the breath of life.

"Then the Lord God formed man of dust from the ground and
breathed into his nostrils the breath of life; and man became a living
being." Genesis 2:7

"He Himself gives to all life and breath and all things, for in Him we
live and move and exist." Acts 17:25-26

Aerobic defined: to move air in and out

We inhale oxygen and exhale carbon monoxide. The respiratory
system is amazing in its efficiency. So is the Spirit's ability to give life to
our human spirit and move out harmful attitudes and habits.

The Holy Spirit is spoken of as the wind.

The Greek word WIND (pneme), means both wind and spirit.

"The wind blows where it wishes and you hear the sound of it, but do not know where it comes from and where it is going; so is everyone who is born of the Spirit." John 3:8

The human soul yielded to the Spirit of God will live in this world, move about and spread the Good News that Christ is risen from the dead and sits at the right hand of the Father interceding for us.

For the child of God prayer is as necessary for our spirit as oxygen is to the human body.

The child of God is saved from hell for eternity and saved from our sinful self-will in this world we live in. The result is that we will be sanctified or set apart for service.

The Holy Spirit intercedes for us and it is our "work" to intercede for others. We are not to bypass our mind. His Spirit will engage our mind and inspire us to do the will of the Father.

"I have been crucified with Christ; and it is no longer I who live, but Christ lives in me; and the life which I now live by faith in the Son of God, who loved me, and delivered Himself up for me (in my place)." Galatians 2:20

So, if salvation is a gift from God then why would we try to work our way into His "good graces". We already have His good grace.

"Foolish Galatians who has bewitched you?" . . . "Having begun by the Spirit, are you now being perfected by the flesh?" Galatians 3:1a and 3:3b

The word of God says to test the spirit/wind to see if it is of God.

"We are no longer children, tossed here and there by waves, and carried about by every wind of doctrine, by trickery of men, by craftiness in deceitful scheming." Ephesians 4:14

Dear Lord God, I pray we become a breath of fresh air to those who long for Your touch. Amen

WATER

Both the body and the spirit must be hydrated. The body with H2O. The human spirit, our inmost being, with the spiritual water Jesus offered the women at the well.

"Whoever drinks of the water that I (Jesus) shall give him shall never thirst, but the water that I shall give him shall become in him a well of water springing up to eternal life," John 4:14

"He who believes in Me, . . ., from his inmost being shall flow rivers of living water." John 7:38

NUTRIENTS ABTAINED

Both the body and the spirit of man must be nourished. One with vitamins and minerals, the other with the Word of God.

"Your words were found, and I ate them, and Your words became to me a joy and the delight of my heart." Jeremiah 15:16

Just like we must go to the grocery store or grow our own food so must we prayerfully go to the Bible for our daily Bread of Life. In Isaiah 55:1 the prophet says something puzzling to the English reader.

Our Lord says to us, "Ho! Everyone who thirsts **come** to the water; and you who have no money **come**, buy and eat. **Come**, buy wine and milk without money and without price." (emphases added)

Clearly, he is speaking of spiritual nourishment. In order for any purchase to happen an exchange must take place. If we buy without money, then someone must pay the price. He tells us to come and keep on coming. It takes self-control to keep coming and not give in to discouragement. Holy Spirit says come to encourage us. It is as though the prophet says, "So, you have no money? No problem! Your faith in Jesus fulfills your part of the transaction."

In our modern vernacular we might say of something that seems too good to be true; "I don't buy it" which means "I don't believe it."

It is our privilege to "buy" or believe the unfathomable. The miracle of the ages is the exchange that takes place between the sinless holy Savior and sinful unholy mankind. The righteous One died for the unrighteous and we are the recipients of His gracious offer. Just as the purchase of literal food at a grocery store is an act of faith that it will contain the nutrients our bodies need; so, it is with the Spiritual food and drink we are provided. Remember the story of the woman at the well; Jesus said that there was food the disciples did not know about. He said; "My food is to do the will of Him who sent Me, and to accomplish His work." It was living water that she did not need to purchase because Jesus gave it to her. All she had to do was believe. She digested the information, communed with Him and received the blessed hope. So, unless we consume the "words of life" and digest/meditate on them our daily walk will be hindered. We would not willingly starve our bodies. Why would we starve ourselves spiritually?

The world, the flesh of man, and the devil thrive on our spiritual malnutrition and spiritual stagnation.

The spirit of man is in need of daily renewal. When it is thin and undernourished it has little chance of implementing God's will. To be sure the overfed soul will call the shots.

"Whoever has no rule over his own spirit is like a city broken down, without walls." Prov. 25:28 NKHV

God's plan is for us to have our identity based on His plan built up in His most Holy grace. And His will that we have boundaries that protect us from exploitation.

Underworld defined: The unseen workings of evil spirit beings. They are always in search of vulnerable people to deceive. Christians are of special attraction to them because we are Christ's representatives in the world.

A persons' spirit should rule over the soul. It requires problems, challenges and testing to subdue the fleshly soul. That is why self-control, (spirit ruling over soul in communion and in obedience to His Spirit) is the last of nine fruits of the Spirit. (Galatian's 5:22)

WASTE RELEASED

This body God created has an incredible ability to absorb nutrition from food and release the waste along with toxins that we inevitably obtain from this fallen world. Human cells grow, release waste, divide and reproduce cells after their own kind.

So it is with the spirit of mankind. We have been given by God a deep desire for love and acceptance. If we yield ourselves to the Great Physician His still small voice will coordinate with the written word and accomplish what only He can. He will merge His thoughts with our thoughts. In this way His plans come into our lies.

"He saves us, not on the basis of deeds which we have done in righteousness, but according to His mercy, by the washing of regeneration and renewing by the Holy Spirit, whom He poured out upon us richly through Jesus Christ our Savior." Titus 3:5-6

Regeneration defined: a new nature and a new life that lasts for all eternity

Renewing defined: the transforming process of the inner man becoming the new self by walking in the Spirit day by day; receiving true knowledge from the Creator. (Romans 12:2, 2 Corinthians 4:6, Colossians 3:10 paraphrased)

"Let all bitterness and wrath and anger and clamor and slander be put away from you, along with all malice. And be kind to one another. Tender-hearted, forgiving each other, just as God in Christ also has forgiven you." Ephesians 4: 31-32

His indwelling does not ebb and flow. He said very plainly that He would never leave us. But our spirits availability and usefulness depend on our moment by moment yieldedness to Him.

Those things that He purges out of our life make room for the filling of His Precious Holy Spirit.

LIFE IS TIME AND TIME IS LIFE

What a "waste" of time to hold on to the toxic emotions of anger, fear, resentment and bitterness. Those things don't hurt the object of our scorn. For the child of God, these things are stumbling blocks and a hindrance to our experiencing the fullness of our spiritual inheritance.

The gifts of God are to be prized above all else – they are temporal, and they are eternal.

It is His desire to give us HIS love.

I Corinthians 13:13

"But now abide faith, hope, love
these three;
but the greatest of these is LOVE."

POSITIONING - STABILITY - COORDINATION
YEILD AND AGREE

The connective tissue of the body gives positioning to the muscles and joints for mobility, stability and coordination. Remember, when the surface under our feet shifts slightly, we can recalibrate and stay upright in an instant before the brain has time to think about what happened.

The human soul under God's control gives us a position of humble obedience to the Spirit of God. When the world seems to shift under our feet He is always near and is making intercession on our behalf.

For a child of God our eternal position is secure from the moment we agree with God and accept the Savior's offer of salvation.

When the human spirit that was dead in its sins comes to life; it will work the way God intended it to. Our position will be of one who lives an exchanged life. The security He offers is ours; right here and right now. We will be single minded and stable.

STABILITY

The soul under fleshly influence puts us in a place where sin feels normal. We will be, "Double minded and unstable in all its ways." James 1:8

He will shake that which needs to be shaken for our good.

He will shake our faith in our own virtue.

But when the connection between our spirit and Gods Spirit is sure and certain the flow will cause us to be able to experience stability as we walk out the troubles of daily life and the sufferings we experience on this mortal soil.

"My soul waits in silence for God only;
From Him is my salvation.
He only is my rock and my salvation.
My stronghold; I shall not be greatly shaken." Psalm 62:1-2

He will not test us beyond our ability to withstand it.

"Therefore, since we receive a kingdom which cannot be shaken, let us show gratitude by which we may offer to God an acceptable service with reverence and awe. For our God is a consuming fire." Hebrews 12:28-29 NOW WE SEE IN A MIRROR DIMLY – WHEN WE SEE HIM, WE WILL BE LIKE HIM

1 Corinthians 13:12 and 1 John 3:2 (My paraphrase)

Until the day we see him the observations we make may be flawed and lacking in authenticity but our gratitude for insight will only lead to a blessing if it leads us to worship Him. He will take our misconceptions and use them as opportunity to teach us blessed truths.

The physical world around us mirrors the God who created it. He knew we would benefit greatly when we see a beautiful sunset or observe a colorful butterfly. Something inside us wants to speak words that declare our fascination.

Even an atheist cannot deny the pleasure of observing the beauty of creation. A spectator's joy is not complete unless they express it in words. In that way, the speaker and the listener participate in the joy of sharing their amazement.

What I have just described to you is a form of worship.

Some people worship the creation but do not worship the Creator. The need to worship someone or something is as necessary to our spirit as breathing air is necessary to our lungs.

COORDINATION

God's plan for the body is that the other five senses yield to the connective tissue in a way that brings rhythm. It facilitates but does not force the coordination of the whole body.

Gods plan is that the soul of man serves the human spirit that is yielded to the Spirit of God.

When the mind is controlled by our fleshly imagination our desires are fed by the world; not God. Our wishing even for "good" things can distract us from God. And our emotions will master us.

We must be careful with the terminology "Choose Christ." He requires that we yield to Him. The words to choose could imply that we have other options and that we are doing Him a favor by "choosing" Him above the others. Choosing to yield, on the other hand, declares and proclaims our utter poverty. To be sure, God does give us the option to choose how we will live out the reality of a life yielded to Him.

Before we can yield to Him, we must agree with
His declaration of our true condition.

Our foolish hearts were darkened, and we were dead in our trespasses and sins making it impossible for us to yield to Christ. But make no mistake, we will yield ourselves to someone or something. Once yielded to an idol, very subtle agreements will fall in place. For a child of God, the shaking He allows will reveal the agreements and break the bondage they cause. He chastens those He loves.

When Adam and Eve sinned in the Garden of Eden, sin entered mankind. The GOOD NEWS is that Jesus made a way for us to be restored to the fellowship of the Garden before the fall. It will not be fully experienced by us until we enter heaven but, in the meantime, yielding to God becomes a way of life and the spirit resumes its purpose as if the barrier to worship does not exist. It is our duty and our pleasure to yield, yield, and yield again until the human soul is in rhythm with the Holy Spirit of God within us.

The blessed result of this union of the natural spirit and supernatural Spirit is that we begin to "walk – by – the – Spirit". Self-conscious awareness melts away and Christ awareness takes its place. We cannot work to bring this miraculous substitution about any more than we can command the body senses to work for us. In fact, if we try to overcome self-awareness in our own self-styled way it will only become stronger.

"If we live by the Spirit, let us also walk by the Spirit." Galatians 5:25

If we yield our members to the Righteous One; "Out
of us shall flow rivers of living water." John 7:38

Our God given senses enable our ability to think, make decisions
and express emotion. The human spirit conveys information to and from
God's Spirit.

When we submit to His Spirit, we are in fact saying to our Lord; "Let
the dance begin."

It's okay if we step on His toes from time to time.
"Love covers a multitude of sins." I Peter 4:8

My paraphrase – His love makes our missteps look like part of the
dance. His skill as a leader is un- paralleled and full of mercy.

Dear Lord, you are the Creator. You redeem our blunders. Yes Lord,
I agree that You are in charge. I know it's true, but I can't see You with
my human eyes. I do see Your handiwork and I am amazed. I sense Your
presence when my sin does not blur my spirit's vision. I hear Your voice
when I'm dialed into Your frequency. I am filled with Your Spirit when
I'm not too full of myself. Your touch of faith, hope, worship, prayer and
love are always available when I am yielded to You. Thank You Lord, You
do not require perfection from us. What You do require is that we," Do
justice, love kindness and walk humbly with our God." Micah 6:8 (My
paraphrase) Thank You for the desire, the motivation, and the strength to
finish well. Thank You for the desire to do Your will. AMEN

"I will give thanks to Thee, for I am fearfully
and wonderfully made." Psalms 139:14a

Our bodies are full of wonders
that cause us to ponder our Creator
with awe and reverence.

Selah – pause and think on these things.

CHAPTER 13

THE STORIES OF JOB AND JERIMIAH

The story of Job in the Bible describes a man whose senses had been bombarded by misfortune even though he had not chosen to go to a far country and take pleasure in loose living.

The book of Job stands alone in its form and theme. It is unique and it addresses an age-old question. If God is good and just why does He allow people to suffer who have done nothing to deserve it?

As human standards are measured, Job is a very good man, yet calamity overwhelms him. He loses his wealth, his ten children all die tragically, and his physical health is in shambles. He loses everything except his life and his wife. Few humans have suffered like Job.

Job's initial response was to worship God.

He said, "Naked I came from my mother's
womb. And naked I shall return there.
The Lord gave and the Lord has taken away.
Blessed be the name of the Lord.
Through all this Job did not sin nor did he blame God." Job1: 21-22

The book of Job is set in the days of the patriarchs before the priesthood or organized religion. The consensus of the day was that prosperity was God's reward for good living and that calamity was God's judgement on the sin of the person.

Job's so called "friends," Eliphaz, Bildad and Zophar took a general truth and made it into a rigid rule.

The words they spoke to Job revealed the hardness of their hearts. They were convinced that their "theology" was more important than Job's own word about his integrity; more important than having compassion for a suffering man.

People in Job's day did not have the advantage of the written word that predicted the sinless suffering Savoir. Nor did they have the prophecy of His actual death, burial and resurrection. These truths might have given Job's accusers reason to doubt their assessment of Job's predicament.

I am only guessing, but I suspect that Jobs suffering made them personally uncomfortable and fearful. If a good man like Job could suffer and it was not because of his sin, then their "theology" was flawed. They could not rest if their belief was false. They managed to find boundaries reminiscent of Scott Peck's stage two spiritual stagnation.

They overwhelmed Job's sense of hearing with words of accusation. Instead of having true dialogue with Job they refused to listen and dug in deeper and deeper. They have become his tormentors, leveling false accusations and offering no answer to his desperate questions.

When an impasse was reached and in his darkest moments faith and hope do well up inside Job. He will not perjure himself and deny his integrity but something inside him changes. He addresses his accusers and says with indignation, "What counsel have you given to one without wisdom!

> What helpful insight you have abundantly provided!
> To whom have you uttered words?
> And whose spirit was expressed through you?" Job 26:3b-4

Job rightly questions whether an evil spirit was prompting them to speak as they had spoken. Then he goes on to declare his innocence.

He said to them, "For as long as life is in me, and
the breath of God is in my nostrils,
My lips certainly will not speak unjustly, nor
will my tongue multiply deceit.
Far be it from me that I should declare you
right; till I die I will not put away
my integrity from me. I hold fast my righteousness and will not let it go.
My heart does not reproach any of my days." Job 27:3-6

God Speaks to Job

As God would have it, and at the proper time in his
tribulation, God initiates dialogue with Job.
Job had imagined himself putting his case to God
and asking His questions. Instead, God asks Job questions.
**Are we beginning to see a pattern here? God spoke
to him first. God asked him questions.
Covenant prayer is two-way conversation
with God Himself leading the way.**

God skillfully puts Job in his place. He realizes that he had been dabbling into things far beyond his understanding. Jobs' questions remained unanswered, but he is satisfied anyway. He realized that understanding isn't all cracked up to be and he realizes that embracing the mystery of life is a better way to live.

Job had an honest seeking heart. But his friends would not allow for truth being bigger than their understanding. They had misrepresented God and they had misjudged Job as guilty of sin worthy of punishment.

The dialogue between God and Job is a perfect example of God reasoning with man. In his day the prophet Isaiah spoke for God when he said, "Come let us reason together, though your sins be as scarlet they shall be white as snow." Is. 1:18

My paraphrase: Let's talk! I will speak first and then I will listen to you. If you are honest with Me this exchange will change your life. Humble repentance will follow. Forgiveness will fill your heart with pure clean gratitude.

Remember, Gods words come with clarity, power, majesty and glory. They will not return void. They are not empty lifeless words.

I praise You Oh Lord. Your word will NOT come back to you without breathing Life to the listener. Your words will do the work, fulfill Your purpose and they will return with validation to the one that watches and waits. Amen

It is very important to note that when Job accepts his suffering and prays **for** his friends God increases his worldly possessions twofold and God gives him ten more children.

Every story of tragedy does not have such a happy ending. But this age we live in is only the beginning. The age to come will be glorious beyond our imagination.

It is not that God trusts anything in the natural man, but He knows with what He can entrust us. In His omnipotence God knew that there would come a moment when Job would embrace a concept of God that was much larger, grander and closer to Reality.

The same was not true of his accusers. In Job 42:7 God rebukes them:

"My anger burns against you and against your two friends
for you have not spoken of Me what is right, as my servant Job has."

Job's suffering did not square with their pre-conceived idea of God as a well-meaning and benevolent taskmaster/cop kind of god.

When Job was sorely tested all his senses cried out in pain. His mind strained to comprehend his misfortune. His human desire was to have his life back like it had been. He was perplexed to the point of despairing, but he never lost his love for God. In the end, he recognized God's voice, his spiritual eyes were opened to see God's Sovereignty, he discerned Truth and felt the touch of God's love and compassion.

God's Words to Job Job 38:1-7
"Then the Lord answered Job out of the whirlwind and said,
Who is this that darkens counsel by words without knowledge?
Now gird up your loins like a man, and I will
ask you, and you instruct Me!
Where were you when I laid the foundations of the earth?

Tell Me, if you have understanding, who set
its measurements, since you know?
Or who stretched the line on it? On what were its bases sunk?
Or who laid its cornerstone when the morning stars sang together,
And all the sons of God shouted for joy?"

Yes, God put him in his place but what a wonderful place He put him in!

"What is man, that Thou dost care for him? Yet
Thou hast made him a little lower than God,
and dost crown him with glory and majesty! Psalm 8:4b-5

After we have settled the issue of Gods loving kindness - then and only
then do we look at problems and testing in a different way.

Job's Repentance Job 42:1-6

"Then Job answered the Lord, and said, I
know that Thou canst do all things,
And that no purpose of Thine can be thwarted. Who
is this that hides counsel without knowledge?
Therefore I have declared that which I did not
understand, things too wonderful for me,
which I did not know. Hear, now, and I will speak;
I will ask Thee and do Thou instruct me.
I have heard of Thee by the hearing of the
ear; but now my eye sees Thee;
therefore I retract, and I repent in dust and ashes."

Job's anxiety was relieved when he acknowledged that God can do anything He purposes to do. His supposed need for God to consult him has vanished. Job's pride was revealed as he yielded to the God he loved.

Remember, when we trust Him; He will entrust us with wonderful knowledge at the perfect time.

In verses 7 and 8 God refers to Job as His servant four times. He had become twice the servant he was before his dark night of the soul.

At one point Job said that he wished he had never been born but later he said, "Though He slay me, I will I hope in Him." Job 13:15

Job said I will hope in Him even if He takes my life from me. (My paraphrase)

You are probably saying this is a very interesting story but what does it have to do with me?

Haven't we all at some time in our lives said, "This is too much for me. I can't take it anymore." We could find ourselves feeling like we are losing our faith. Possibly it is our "religious attitudes" we need to lose.

He relinquished his claim to himself and laid claim to his God. It is as though he said, "If I perish, I perish, but I will not even attempt to receive deliverance from anyone except God because there is no such deliverance."

Hope that is settled and sure, even when circumstances are difficult, is faith in its purest form. This kind of faith will not disappoint.

"How long will you hesitate between two opinions? If the Lord is God, follow Him; but if Baal, follow him." 1 Kings 18:21

Romans 10:11,13 "Whoever believes in Him will not be disappointed. Whoever will call upon the name of the Lord will be saved."

My salvation is a settled issue, so I do not hope for something I already have. I should hope for something I need more of.

Lord, this moment I hope for clarity from you, closeness to you
and assurance that the deepest desires of my heart will be granted
in Your time, in Your way and in rhythm
with the beat of Your heart. Amen

There was another great man of faith that can give us insight into the workings of God and how we can appropriate Gods strength to keep on walking down the road with our Lord.

Jeremiah is called the weeping prophet. He cried out from his own Job-like experience.

God's Sovereignty is experienced and expressed by these two men in very different ways. Job was a man of integrity accused of things he did not do. Jeremiah was also a man of integrity who God called to accuse a rebellious nation of things they most certainly had done. In both instances God's Sovereignty is brought into question.

"Who is in charge – God or man?"

THE STORY OF JEREMIAH – HIS CALL – HIS COMMISION

God spoke through His prophet Jeremiah. He said," Before I formed you in the womb I knew you, and before you were born I consecrated you, I have anointed you prophet to the nations." Jeremiah 1:5

He started his prophetic journey at about the age of twenty and spent forty years walking out a very lonely existence. God assigned Jeremiah the task of prophesying both destruction and blessing. It is almost impossible to make friends when you are assigned the task of speaking words of rebuke. He was imprisoned and often in danger of losing his life. He grieved over the stubborn refusal of his people to repent of their idolatry. Despite his sensitivity and lack of self-confidence he did not compromise the message from God. There is a strand of hope in his words because he knew that their God was a God of mercy. He kept telling them in so many words; "After you have experienced God's judgement and exile in Egypt you will be restored to the joy of the Lord and prosper in your homeland" (My paraphrase)

> "For thus says the Lord, "When seventy years have been completed for Babylon, I will visit you and fulfill My good word to you, to bring you back to this place. For I know the plans that I have for you, declares the Lord, plans for welfare and not for calamity to give you a future and a hope. Then you will call upon Me, and come and pray to Me, and I will listen to you. And you will seek Me and find Me, When you search for Me with all your heart." Jeremiah 29:10-13

Jeremiah proclaimed that after seventy years of exile in Egypt they would return to their land a changed people. Those of us alive today look forward to the final fulfillment. In Jeremiah's day this proclamation was fulfilled. There will be complete restoration of the Jews in their land after the great tribulation yet to come upon the earth and in the Millennial Kingdom that Jesus will establish after those days of judgement.

> Romans 11:25-27 "For I do not want you brethren, to be uninformed of this mystery, lest you be wise in your own

estimation, that a partial hardening has happened to Israel until the fulness of the Gentiles, has come in; and thus all Israel will be saved"

"The Deliverer will come from Zion. He will remove ungodliness from Jacob. And this is My covenant with them, when I take away their sins." Quoted from Isaiah 59:20-21

Let's go back to Jeremiah's day.

What did God say through His prophet Jerimiah that enraged the people so much?

First, he repeatedly proclaimed;" The **word** of the Lord came to me."

Second, that **word** proclaimed that they were substituting ritualistic sacrifice for obedience.

Third, the **word** he spoke proclaimed that they were worshiping idols and that the scribes, false prophets and priests did nothing that did not suit their own self-interest.

No wonder he was the least popular man in the country. But he is in good company. Jesus Himself received the same kind of hatred from many of the people and the religious leaders of His day.

Even though Jerimiah was sorely hated he did not soften his words of rebuke nor did he stop reminding the people of Israel that God was grieved by their rejection of Him and the inevitable consequences that were to come. Jeremiah kept telling them that God was willing to restore them if they would repent.

Even in the middle of judgement, God does not lose sight of individuals. When Jeremiah is worn out and about at the end of his rope the Lord speaks to him directly concerning his personal distress.

At times Jeremiah felt that God had failed him. The following passage reveals his honest discouragement and Gods gracious answer.

Jerimiah 15:15-18a, 19-21

"Thou who knowest, O Lord, remember me, take notice of me, and take vengeance for me on my persecutors. Do not, in view of Thy patience, take me away; know that for Thy sake I endure reproach. Thy words were found and I ate them, and Thy words became for me a joy and the delight of my heart; for I have been called by Thy name, O Lord God of hosts. I did not sit in the circle of merrymakers, nor did I exult. Because of Thy hand upon me I sat alone, for thou didst fill me with indignation. Why has my pain been perpetual and my wound incurable, refusing to be healed?"

God's answer to Jerimiah's cry of lonely despair:

"Therefore, thus says the Lord, <u>if you return, then I will restore you</u>- Before Me you will stand; and if you extract the precious from the worthless, you will become My spokesman. They for their part may turn to you, but <u>as for you, you must not turn to them</u>. Then I will make you to this people a fortified wall of bronze; and though they fight against you, they will not prevail over you; for I am with you to save you and deliver you from the hand of the wicked, and I will redeem you from the grasp of the violent."(emphases added)

The apostle James put it this way, "Submit to God, resist the devil and he will flee from you," (James 4:7) The Spirit of God did spoke the same truth to him words he needed to hear and at the exact moment he needed to hear them.

The prophet was a mere mortal just like we are. He was tested in all the ways we are tested. But even beyond that, the Lord put restrictions on him that most of us will never know. He was forbidden to marry, take part in funerals or happy social occasions.

It would have been much easier for him to identify with his fellow humans, with their faults and failures. He was a tenderhearted man. But God spoke very clearly to him when He said," you must not turn to them."

I'm sure they could have made a convincing argument explaining and justifying their rebellion. If he had allowed himself the luxury of sympathy, he would have become a hindrance and a barrier to their repentance.

If he had given in to his inclination to have compassion and allowed that inclination to take root, he would have missed his God given calling.

To identify with his fellow humans, sympathize with them and gain their approval would have been the path of least resistance. Bucking society and becoming an outcast was the path of most resistance.

Jerimiah did not have the blessing of Jesus' admonition in the book of Luke Chapter 6; "Blessed are you when men hate you, and ostracize you, and cast insults at you and spurn your name as evil, for the sake of the son of Man. Be glad in that day, and leap for joy; for behold your reward is great in heaven; for in the same way their fathers used to treat the prophets." Verses 22-23

Nor did he have the advantage of the indwelling Spirit, but He did have the Spirit's words come upon him with grace and power to obey.

There are two paths before all of us.

The path of least resistance exposes us to a life typified by rebellion that separates us from the love of God and offers no protection from Gods judgement. For the child of God living as a mere convert is typified by no fruit or manmade fake fruit. The path of most resistance comes with Gods promise of protection from the perils of the path that seems safer to our human senses. One thing for sure, as long as we are sitting by the side of the road, we will never have our path corrected. Those corrections move us toward our destiny. We must stay active to His leading.

To identify with the ways and desires of God Almighty takes a miracle.

That miracle is the exchanged life.

"It is not I that live but Christ that lives in me." Galatians 2:20

Resistance Becomes Restoration

The Lord placed before Jerimiah two choices. First, He said if you return to Me, I will restore you. He clearly had not left the country so what did the Lord mean by return? Later verses reveal the answer to that question. He said even if the people turn to you; you must not turn to them. I believe our Lord did not want Jerimiah to become obsessed with the acceptance of his countrymen.

Paul's advice to us in Ephesians 6:6 is to live like slaves of Christ; not in order to please men but to please God by doing His will from the heart. (my paraphrase)

The word addiction gets used a lot these days.

It is said that people are addicted to shopping or gambling.

To be sure there are addictions, but I think the word obsessed might be the better word to describe most of us.

We are all obsessed with someone or something. Often our obsessions are focused on good things and sometimes they are focused on worthless things. There are the things we know we should do but refuse to do even though we know they are God's will for us. They are the so-called sins of omission. Other times our obsessions are sins of commission. Either way, when we are rigid in our heart desires God will eventually have to remold us.

Jerimiah 18:1-6,10

"The word which came to Jerimiah from the Lord saying, Arise and go down to the potter's house, and there I shall announce My words to you. Then I went down to the potter's house, and he was, making something on the wheel. But the vessel that he was making of clay was spoiled in the hand of the potter; so, he remade it into another vessel, as it pleased the potter to make. Then the word of the Lord came to me saying, Can I not, O house of Israel, deal with you as this potter does? declares the Lord. Behold, like clay in the potter's hand, so are you in My hand, O house of Israel. . .. If (that nation Israel) does evil in My sight by not obeying My voice, then I will think better of the good with which I had promised to bless it."

In verse 11 the Lord pleads with the people to repent. He said, "Behold, I am fashioning calamity against you and devising a plan against you. Oh, turn back, each of you from his evil way, and reform your ways and your deeds."

He clearly would rather not send judgement, but He loves them and does what He must do to return them to fellowship with Himself.

In Jeremiah 29:11-13 the Lord makes it very clear exactly the plans He wants for His people; plans for welfare and hope with which He had promised to bless them. But He will not force them to worship Him and by extension chose His plan.

"Declares the Lord, Plans for welfare and not
for calamity to give you a future and a hope."

Second, the Lord said to Jerimiah, "If you will extract the precious
from the worthless you will become My spokesman and you will be
protected by My mighty hand." Jeremiah 15:19 (My paraphrase)

"Oh, the depth of the riches both of the knowledge of God! How
unsearchable are His judgements and unfathomable His ways!" Romans
11:33-36

Jerimiah was given the choice to resist the temptation to be obsessed
with things worth far less and suffer loss for his short time on earth or to
be obsessed with the mighty God of the universe, fulfill his calling, and
receive his reward in eternity.

What things or people do you treasure above all else?

"Where your treasure is there will your heart be also." Matthew 6:21

"You shall love the Lord your God with all your heart, and with all
your soul and with all your mind." . . . "You shall love your neighbor as
yourself." Matthew 22: 37-39b

That sounds like an obsession to me; an obsession never to be
repented of.

May it never be that we abandon our Lord after we have tasted His
words of joy and delight.

If your heart is right with God, you will find a treasure chest full of
blessings.

"I urge you therefore brethren, by the mercies of God, to present your
bodies a holy sacrifice, acceptable to God, which is your spiritual service
of worship. And do not be conformed to the world, but be transformed by
the renewing of your mind, that you may prove what the will of God is
that which is good and acceptable and perfect." Romans 12:1-2

Order Is Very Important to Our God
Order is the Opposite of Chaos

If the Lord is our treasure, He will put the wonderful blessings He
gives us into their proper order. Some of the lesser things we obsess about

will seem to fall away but others seem only to go out by the crucible. Jesus said for us to take up our cross/crucible and follow Him. Problems and testing serve their purpose in our lives to perfect and bless us.

Job's tormentors were obsessed with the doctrine of; do good, be good and get good things from God.

Jerimiah's tormentors were obsessed with; do bad, be bad and get good things from God anyway.

In both instances, their ears were not listening to God. They were only hearing the lies of the world and they were being molded to match that which they were obsessed. Their hearts were hard toward the Lord God Almighty.

Parable of the soils - Metaphor of soil for ears. Mark 4:9 Living The Message - Eugene Peterson

"What is the quality of my hearing? Are my ears thick with calluses, impenetrable like a heavily trafficked path? Are my ears superficially attentive like rocky ground in which everything germinates but nothing takes root? Are my ears like an indiscriminate weed patch in which the noisy and repetitive take up all the space without regard for truth, quality, beauty, or fruitfulness? Or are my ears good soil which readily receives God's word, well-tilled to welcome deep roots, to discriminately choose God's word and reject the lies of the world."

The physical heart beats with a rhythm. The spiritual heart beats also and it is either a self-prescribed "beat to a different drummer" or we are listening with ears attentive to His voice and His order.

He will be as gentle as possible but if we persist in ignoring His calling, he will have to convince us that His love is greater, grander and more desirable than any other love.

HOLY SPIRIT – CONVICTS OF SIN

He is the "Convincer I Chief"

Someone once said, "I have Jesus. Jesus is all I need." That is true! But life has to convince us of it. If a person will not be convinced that Jesus is the Messiah, it is because of their rebellion; not because the Holy Spirit lacks the powers of persuasion. Persuasion is not coercion. There is an old hymn that uses the term "almost persuaded." If we maintain an ALMOST mentality, it is not Gods fault if we go to hell when we die.

John 5:24 ESV says; "Truly, truly, I say to you, whoever hears my word and believes Him who sent me has eternal life. He does not come into judgement but has passed from death to life."

Lord, Lord . . . many will say in that day, "Didn't I do all these things in Your name"? But You will say, "Depart from Me. I never knew you." Matthew 7:23 (my paraphrase)

There is a pathway that seems right to a man but in the end it's a road to death. Proverbs 14:12 ISV

From that statement it is obvious that our opinions are not reliable. But it comes natural to us to come up with a scheme to try and "beat the rap".

JESUS WILL JUDGE THE UNBELIEVER

At the Great White Throne, after the one thousand years of the millennium kingdom, Jesus will judge those who have shown by their works that they deserve eternal punishment in the lake of fire. They will be resurrected to hear their "formal sentencing."

Redemption is available to all men as far as paying the price for sin is concerned. (2 Peter 2:1 paraphrased)

The death of Christ is not lacking in its value. But His death is only effective for the elect. It is applied only the those who believe is His death, burial and resurrection.

To put it in common terms; a gift can be purchased and presented by the giver in only those who see value in the gift and received it with gratitude will be counted among the believers in Christ and experience the blessings of salvation.

THERE ARE THREE KINDS OF JUDGEMENT
FOR BELIEVERS IN JESUS CHRIST

The first is self-judgement.

1 Corinthians 11:28 says;" Let a man examine himself."

The contrast between ourselves and Jesus will lead us to the conclusion that we are in desperate need of a savior.

The second kind of judgement is disciplinary.

In Hebrews 12:9-11, Paul tells us what we need to know about this kind of discipline.

"We had earthly fathers to discipline us, and we respected them shall we not much rather be subject to the Father of spirits and live? For they disciplined us for a short time as seemed best to them, but He disciplined us for our good, that we may share His holiness. All discipline for the moment seems not to be joyful but sorrowful, yet to those who have been trained by it, afterwards it yields the peaceful fruit of righteousness."

When Christians get off tract His discipline restores us to the right path. It is part of our educational process and it proves the Fathers love for His children. He wants us to return, repent and have our relationship restored.

"Trust in the Lord with all your heart . . . My son, do not reject the discipline of the Lord." Proverbs 3:5a,11a

And what does our Lord say about those who accept discipline and commit their lives to Him?

"I will be merciful to their iniquities, And I will remember their sins no more." Hebrews 8:12

The third kind of judgement is the Bema Seat Judgement of Christ.

It is a time of reward for valuable works done at the Spirits leading and "house cleaning" for past behaviors that are worthless. It is the quality of works that is being judged NOT the person. This will happen after the rapture of the church and before the second coming of Jesus Christ to the earth.

"For we must all appear before the judgement seat {Bema Seat} of Christ that each one may be recompensed for his deeds in the body, according to what he has done, whether good or bad." 2 Corinthians 5:9-10

"If any man's work which he has built upon it remains he shall receive a reward. If any man's work is burned up, he shall suffer loss but he himself shall be saved, yet so as through fire." 1 Corinthians 3:14-15

"Now to Him who is able to keep you from stumbling, and to make you stand in the presence of His glory blameless with great joy, to the only God our Savior, through Jesus Christ our Lord, be glory, majesty, dominion and authority, before all time and now and forever. Amen" Jude 24-25

It will be like high school graduation. Everyone who graduates rejoices and the person in charge of the ceremony rejoices with each graduate.

While we are still here on this earth, we have the
opportunity to bring glory to our Lord.
In His humility, He honors our choices and He
works with whatever we give Him.
A question to be asked is this; what are we giving Him to work with?

Someone once said; "Just because God can make a silk purse out of a sow's ear that does not give us the right to give Him a sow's ear."

Are we giving Him our leftover devotion after we've spent our time, money and talents on our self-interest? Jeremiah's warnings are still relevant. And his encouragements still ring true today if we are willing to be humbled by the skillful hand of God.

MOLDED BY GOD

Clay is an important substance.
a raw material.
When placed in the potters' hand
it becomes a thing of usefulness and beauty.

God's own chosen people He compared to clay.

You are chosen, unique and important.
a work in progress.
gifted and useful to God
when molded by the Masters' plan.

"Just as the clay is in the potters' hand, so are
you in My hand." Jerimiah 18:6

CHAPTER 14

THE MASTERS PLAN FOR OUR LIVES

We are unique individuals created by God to fulfill our divine destiny. The problem is the sin nature we all inherited from our mutual ancestor Adam the First. Isn't it just like God to use life problems to deal with the original problem of sin?

No one knows our sin nature better than God and He knows each of us individually. His plan for us is a uniquely personal plan but His goals are universal.

One of Gods Goals: To bring us into a spiritual place where we can worship Him in spirit and in truth.

HIS WORD IS TRUTH

Our Bible teaches us that God's words have power. God said, "Let there be light; and there was light." Genesis 1:3

In the New Testament, there is the glorious statement that refers to Jesus as the Word; "In the beginning was the Word and the Word was God." John 1:1

Michael Wells said that we Christians suffer because we do not correctly define our words. I would agree and add that we also suffer when we ignore the divine order of God's word to us.

1 Corinthians 15:45-47

> "The first man, Adam BECAME A LIVING SOUL. The
> last Adam (Jesus) became a life-giving spirit. However, the
> spiritual is not first, but the natural; then the spiritual.
> The first man is from the earth, earthly; the second man
> is from heaven."

We are all born with a sin nature first and it is the work of the Holy
Spirit to introduce us to the man from heaven who takes away the sin of
the world.

> Jesus is the beginning of the work of God and
> He is the end, the Alpha and Omega.

We have become very accustomed to the 1,2,3 list of instructions that
come with things we purchase. But Gods order for our individual lives
cannot be systemized, reproduced and published for mass consumption.
Because He is God, He knows the appropriate time for everything and the
precise order necessary to accomplish His desired goal.

Ecclesiastes 3:11 "He has made everything appropriate in its time."
He chooses to reveal certain truths to us only when He knows we are
ready and if we will be blessed for the knowing. We are created to have an
eternal perspective.

> "He has also set eternity in their heart.
> Yet so that man will not find out the work God has done from
> the beginning even to the end." Ecclesiastes 3:11

The eternal perspective will help us look beyond the everyday things
of life, but He does not reveal all of life's mysteries to us.

The people of Jerimiah's day despised the word of God spoken through
the prophet. But Jerimiah embraced Gods plan for his life and found the
blessed peace that only a child of God can know. He wept tears of sorrow
over the things of life that really matter.

Jesus said," . . . Seek first His Kingdom and His righteousness; and all
these things shall be added to you." Matthew 6:33

What were "these things"? In the physical world these things were necessities of life, food, clothing and water. In the spiritual world these things are the calm assurances that God will provide for our needs.

He went on to say; "Therefore do not be anxious for tomorrow; for tomorrow will care for itself. Each day has enough trouble of its own." Matthew 6:34

There is an old song that goes like this:

It takes a worried man to sing a worried song. I'm worried now but I won't be worried long. As the song goes the man had broken the law but he thought he could get away with it. The problem was that he got so tired that he had to rest. While he was asleep the authorities found him and the plan he had for himself was foiled. He had thrown all his energies into avoiding consequences with no thought of his moral condition. If you think of these lyrics as a parable the worried man is like the son who went off to the far country to live out the plan, he had chosen for himself.

"Each day has enough trouble of its own."
The Purpose of Trouble by George Hodges

"Whatever else trouble is in the world for, it is here for this good purpose: to develop strength. For trouble is a moral and spiritual task. It is something which is hard to do. And it is in the spiritual world as in the physical, strength is increased by encounter with the difficult. A world without any trouble in it would be, to people of our kind, a place of spiritual enervation and moral laziness. Fortunately, every day is crowded with care. Each day to every one of us brings its questions, its worries, and its tasks, brings its sufficiency of trouble. Thus, we get our daily spiritual exercise."

"The toughness it takes to face life and the formidable reverses which it brings to us can come only through the discipline of endurance and hardship. In His mercy and love our Master makes this a part of our program. It is part of the price of belonging to Him." (closed quote)

Another of God's Goals for Our Lives: To settle the issue of His lovingkindness and our surrender to His Sovereignty.

A Shepherd Looks at the 23<u>rd</u> Psalm by Phillip Keller

"We may rest assured that He will never expect us or ask us to face more than we can stand. (1 Corinthians 10:13) But what He does expose us to will strengthen and fortify our faith and confidence in His control. If He is the Good Shepherd, we can rest assured that He knows what He is doing. This in and of itself should be sufficient to continually refresh and restore my soul. I know of nothing which so quiets and enlivens my own spiritual life as the knowledge that – "God knows what He is doing with me"! (close quote)

If He miraculously resolved all our problems before we are focused on His generosity and compassion, we would "spend" His grace on our pleasures. We would take pleasure in what we judge to be our own self- sufficiency and that would work against us. I suspect He withholds (keeps back and saves) some blessings until we are ready or until someone we love is ready.

Our daily spiritual exercise consists of choices we make every day. God highly values our choices. When we look at the lives of men in the Bible their lives were not always shining examples of virtue. Their stories are told with honesty and their failures are not whitewashed. The value of their choices lies in the opportunity for God to establish Himself as the Ruler of their lives. Then and only then could they worship Him in Spirit and in Truth.

If God is humble enough to take what we give Him and use it for our good, then partnering with Him is a privilege we should not take lightly.

Another of God's goals: To exercise us in the area of patience with God's plan.

King David the Master's Man 1 Chronicles Chapter 21

At this period of King David's life, he is an example of one who refused to listen to Gods' prophet. He tested the Lord and witnessed the consequences of his behavior. But God did not banish him into outer darkness. In fact, in the New Testament our Lord spoke this prophetic word, He said that David was; "A man after His own heart, who will do my will." Acts 13:22

In the old testament David's calling was clearly stated. Just like Gideon, God spoke prophetically of the man David would become. He sees future character as clearly as if it already exists.

"The Lord has sought out for Himself a man after His own heart, and the Lord has appointed him as ruler over His people, because you (Saul) have not kept what the Lord commanded you." 1 Samuel 13:14

In His sovereignty He knows the beginning from the end, and He knew that as David went deeper and lower with God his true potential would be revealed. He knew David's natural man would have to be dealt with first and then the spiritual man would be free to grow and prosper.

And again, in Psalm 89:3-4 God's plan for David's life is clearly stated and their covenant relationship is established.

"I have made a covenant with My chosen; I have sworn to David My servant, I will establish your seed forever, and build up your throne to all generations."

David did have many admirable traits like our Lord. He was not passive. Instead, He was aggressive when the situation called for it. He was not intimidated even by the religious leaders of His day. And he was a man of great compassion. But the similarities do end. While David had a lot of those traits his character was flawed. Jesus always waited for the Father's guidance and obeyed Him implicitly. David did not always wait for guidance and even when he had guidance he did not always obey.

According to the account in 1 Chronicles chapter 21, even after Gods prophet warned him against it, David sent out a command across the nation that caused death and destruction. God sent judgement because of David's disobedience. Death and destruction were probably the very things David had hoped to avoid. He did not wait to see God's mighty hand of protection. David's curiosity and impatience back- fired. But God did used David's fleshly choice to bring about the surrender He was after.

The story of King David and the sinful census. 1 Chronicles 21:1-30

God allowed Satan to tempt David to take a census of his people, the Israelites. David wanted to know how many army men he had at his beck and call. The prophet Joab warned him against such an action.

Just like procuring food, clothing and shelter is not a sin neither was taking a census inherently wrong. It was the reason behind David's command that brought about Gods judgement. David was counting on his military might to keep them safe instead of counting on God. He was not dependent on God nor was he surrendered to Gods plan for the safety of the people.

Jehovah Jireh means God will provide. God will see to it. Geneses 22

When Abraham was obedient to God and willing to sacrifice his son; Jehovah Jireh provided a sacrificial lamb to die in Isaac's place. When Abraham took his son up on mount Moriah he did not know how "it" would turn out, but he trusted God to provide the answer.

Our **problem** is that in our lives we do not know what "it" will look like or how long He will take to provide what we really need. Curiosity about the future and impatience to receive what we want are at the root of many a bad decision.

It took about ten months to complete the census. He had all that time to reconsider his decision and pray about it, but he ignored the prophetic warning. He did not seek God's guidance for himself.

1 Chronicles 21:7-8 "And God was displeased with this thing, so He struck Israel. And David said to God, I have sinned greatly, in that I have done this thing. But now, please take away the iniquity of Thy servant, for I have done very foolishly."

Repent defined: to admit a wrong action or attitude, to turn around and go in the opposite direction

God chooses to send judgement.
He spoke through Gad, David's seer and he gave David three choices.

The three choices were either three years of famine, three months while the sword of his enemies overtook them or three days of the sword of the Lord in the form of pestilence through out the land of Israel. David said to Gad; "This is very destressing but I would rather fall into the hand of the Lord because His mercies are very great. But I do not want to fall into the hand of man." (My paraphrase of verses 12,13)

The consequences of our sin often affect other people. King David was no exception. Most of us will never be faced with choices that have the potential to impact so many people and in such a profound way.

Seventy thousand men of Israel died because of his sin.

"And David said to God, is it not I who commended to count the people? Indeed, I am the one who sinned and done very wickedly, but these sheep, what have they done? O Lord my God, please let Thy hand be against me and my father's household, but not against Thy people that they should be plagued." Verse 17

David's opinion of God's merciful nature was correct. At the precise moment God was sending an angel to destroy Jerusalem David chooses to repent again. It was at that exact moment that God chooses to relent and spare the city and its inhabitants.

Relent defined: to respond to repentance with mercy

The Lord is gracious and merciful; slow to anger and great in lovingkindness. Psalm 145:8

As the story draws to a close God tells David to build an alter to the Lord on the threshing floor of Ornan the Jebusite.

"So David went up **at the word of the Lord;**" spoken through Gad. Verse 19

He went up to purchase the land used by Ornan to thresh wheat. Ornan was willing to give it to David for no cost. David said, "No, but I will surely buy it for full price; for I will not take what is yours for the Lord, or offer burnt offering which costs me nothing."

An important principle of sacrifice is that it will cost us something.

Notice that David's repentance was not merely a mental assent. His repentance was demonstrated in action that had its source in the Lord God Almighty. Yes, it cost him something. It cost him money but more importantly it cost him his pride.

While salvation is a free gift that we cannot earn, Philip Keller is right, there is a cost for obeying Him. Christian martyrs have lost their lives but most of are not called to physically die for our faith. We are called to be a living sacrifice. We are called to be expendable; like broken bread and poured out wine.

"The sacrifices of God are a broken spirit; a broken and contrite heart O God, Thou wilt not despise." Psalm 51:17

"I urge you therefore, brethren, by the mercies of God, to present your bodies a living sacrifice and holy sacrifice acceptable to God, which is your spiritual service of worship. And do not be conformed to this world, but be transformed by the renewing of your mind, that you may prove what the will of God is, that which is good and acceptable and perfect." Romans 12:1-2

David did build an alter there and sacrificed burnt offerings and peace offerings to the Lord who commanded His angel to put away his sword.

"To obey is better than sacrifice." 1 Samuel 15:22b

"He (Jesus) learned obedience from the things He suffered." Hebrews 5:8

The difference between Jesus and David's sacrifice is that Jesus did not suffer as a result of His own sin. He was sinless and yet suffering was a part of His life.

David wept and prayed after his sin was exposed but there is no mention of his praying about the census even after he was warned by the prophet.

It would have been better if he had listened to God's man and then prayed for himself. It's much easier to dismiss another human as misguided or just plain wrong. Much earlier the Israelite people had refused to listen to God for themselves. They wanted Moses to go up on the mountain so that they had no direct contact. Obedience seemed optional to them then as it had seemed optional to David.

David spoke of himself as God's servant when he said he had acted very foolishly.

Firstly, he needed to seek the Lord's council and secondly, he needed to serve the Lord with an honest heart; admitting his utter helplessness to rule over the nation of Israel. David had not sought God's Kingdom first. He was too focused on his earthly kingdom and he had been anxious about tomorrow; losing sight of things that really mattered.

God did send judgement after David's disobedience, but the Davidic covenant remains in place to this very day. The covenant with David and his descendants was not bases of David's goodness. It was based on the sovereign will of God. The Father in His perfect omnipotence knew that our Lord would come from the lineage of David. Romans 1:3-4 states that

Jesus was born a descendent of David according to the flesh and declared the Son of God (according to the Spirit). My paraphrase

1 Chronicles 21:25-26 adds even more clarity to the subject of God's everlasting covenant. It states that David bought the whole property where the threshing floor was located. And in 2 Samuel 24:24 we are told that a few years later David's son Solomon built the Temple on this very location. Only the wall of the Temple stands today but David and all his descendants are the rightful owners of the property.

God's Chosen People

"For thou art a holy people unto the Lord thy God; the Lord thy God hath chosen thee to be a special people unto himself; above all people that are on the earth." Deuteronomy 7:6 (KJV)

He chose the Jews to give prophetic words to a lost and suffering world, to write the Bible for all the generations and to reveal the triune God as the Supreme Ruler of the universe.

It did not seem loving and kind to send judgement.
We want to say, "God, what are You doing?"
The truth is that sometimes we must be broken before we can be fixed.

The price to be paid consists of many changes of heart, submitting to the God we love, resisting the devil and denouncing our pride. The reward will be far beyond our wildest expectation. We will receive the restoration which is our spiritual inheritance. We are part of a grand plan. Sometimes that plan will cause us pain. The enemy of our souls will try to get us to focus on the pain and give in to self-pity. God would have us focus on the prize set before us; the joy of His presence to bless and encourage us.

Jesus said, "He who is forgiven little, loves little." Luke 7:47

David certainly was forgiven much. He started out a brave youth who stood up against the giant Goliath. But he went on to become the king of Israel and use his royal position to see to it that his mistresses' husband was sure to die in battle. That same man went on to write some of our most beloved Psalms.

A Psalm of David after Nathan the prophet
confronted him about his sin with Bathsheba.

Psalm 51:10-14,17

"Create in me a clean heart, O God, and renew a steadfast spirit within me. Do not cast me away from Thy presence. And do not take Thy Holy Spirit from me. Restore to me the joy of Thy salvation. And sustain me with a willing spirit. Then I will teach transgressors Thy ways, and sinners will be converted to Thee."

"Deliver me from blood guiltiness, O God, Thou God of my salvation; then my tongue will joyfully sing of Thy righteousness."

"The sacrifices of God are a broken spirit; a broken and a contrite heart, O God Thou wilt not despise." Psalm 51:17

Of course, there are those things in our lives that are not the result of our choice. It is a matter of God's Sovereignty. They come by His choice. So, am I willing to say to Him, "This is what You have given me? I will go down your chosen path. I chose to go prayerfully and willingly."

If His character is displayed in His willingness to hang in there with our character flaws and love us in spite of ourselves then shouldn't we be willing to yield to His eternal perspective and wait for Him?

We are called according to His purpose, so it follows that
the divine order is dependency before surrender.

If we do not have our dependency issues settled, we are likely to surrender to our fleshly desires and seek deliverance from someone other than God.

Another of God's goals: His plan is to give us peace.

Job, Jerimiah, and King David certainly were very different in their approaches to God, but the result was the same. Their willingness to ultimately depend on God's wisdom and surrender their own plan for their lives lead them to a place of peace. They had changes of heart that resulted in the fruit of righteousness. But make no mistake; it was His righteousness imparted and none of their own.

"God causes all things to work together for good to those who love God, to those who are called according to His purpose." Romans 8:28

His purposes are His goals.

King David was tested as to his purposes and his goals. His heart condition was revealed to himself and those around him. God did not need to evaluate David's score on a test. God, in his foreknowledge, knew David's heart.

The test was not the end. It was the beginning of another phase of his journey to that lovely country called; My Pease I Give To You.

After many challenges, failures and successes David was able to speak words to the Lord that we cherish today.

A Prayer of David Psalm 86:1-5,11-13

"Incline Thine ear, O Lord, and answer me; for I am afflicted and needy. Do preserve my soul, for I am a godly man; O thou my God, save Thy servant who trusts in Thee. Be gracious to me, O Lord, for to Thee I cry all day long. Make glad the soul of Thy servant, for to Thee, O Lord, I lift up my soul. For Thou Lord, art good, and ready to forgive and abundant in lovingkindness to all who call upon Thee."

"Teach me Thy way, O Lord; I will walk in Thy truth; unite my heart to fear Thy name. I will give thanks to Thee, O Lord my God, with all my heart, and will glorify Thy name forever. For Thy lovingkindness toward me is great, and Thou hast delivered my soul from the depths of Sheol."

Sheol defined: everlasting separation from God

Forgiving ourselves is one of the "precious things."

Gratitude for receiving forgiveness from God will make it possible for us to forgive ourselves. Self-loathing (another of the hyphenated self-sins) does not help us. In fact, that attitude will hinder our moving on and hinder us from finding our calling. It is an agreement with the enemy that must be repented of. If David had not moved on with God, he would never have been able to write the beloved Psalm 86. God knew he would move on!

GOD ENCOURAGES US – SATAN DIS-COURAGES US

Dear Lord, please come be my courage to move on after moral or spiritual failure. Help my weaknesses. Brave, daring and confident are not words that describe me in my natural state of being. Confidence in You

Lord does not come naturally either. I know it is Satan's desire to kill, steal and destroy my confidence in Your forgiveness. He wants to tear us apart with a negative reversing force.

Lord, please help me remember that any temptation of the enemy, any problem, any loss is allowed by You. You empathize with my pain and You will never leave me or forsake me. You will never waste my affliction. Please give me ears to hear Your instruction. Reveal to me who or what I'm depending on for deliverance. Please bring the splintered parts of my heart into unity with Your plan. Your plans are for my instruction in righteousness, a bright future and hope that doesn't disappoint. Lord, am I childlike enough to be molded by You? Amen

"For the Lord will not abandon His people on account of His great name. (His name signifies His reputation and His character) because the Lord has been pleased to make you a people for Himself." 1 Samuel 12:22 (Explanation added)

Jesus said, "These things I have spoken to you, that in Me you may have peace. In the world you have tribulation but take courage; I have overcome the world." John 16:33

"Peace I leave with you; not as the world gives, do I give to you. Let not your heart be troubled, nor let it be fearful." John 14:2

My faith in God's character pierces the imaginary veil and immediately I am before God Who is making me alive with Him, establishing me in His authority and anointing me with His love and favor. I receive His reward with gratitude, and I give thanks.

"Without faith it is imposable to please God,
For he who comes to God must believe that He is,
And that He is a rewarder of those who seek Him." Hebrews 11:6

CHAPTER 15

PRAYER, OUR HOLY OCCUPATION

Another of God's goals for our lives: to teach us to pray

Remember, the Father created us to be a companion for His Son and to bear spiritual fruit that nourishes other Christians. Together with the Holy Spirit we can spread God's love to a lost world.

This journey we are on together is not for the faint of heart. Possibly that is why so many of us choose the path-of-least resistance, obsess about lesser things or things that don't really matter at all. Could that be why we live a life of defeat?

Some will say, "I tried to be a Christian myself and it just didn't work for me."

Possibly that is because they had not yet realized that there are two selves in each of us!

There were two trees in the garden of Eden. One was the tree of the knowledge of good and evil the other was the tree of life. Correspondingly, there are two selves in each of us.

There is a self to be rejected and a self to be respected.

The fact that there are two selves is clearly outlined in God's word. Matthew addressed the self to be rejected or denied. He said; "If anyone wishes to come after Me, let him deny himself, and take up his cross, and follow Me." Matthew 16:24

The self to be respected is described in the book of Luke. "You shall love the Lord your God with all your heart, and with all your soul, and with all your mind; and your neighbor as yourself." Luke 10:27

After we have become disillusioned with our own supposed virtue; reality sets in. The reality of the person God is making of us begins to emerge. We begin to appreciate the fact that Christ lives in us and He is more than happy to enter into a partnership with us. It saddens Him when we try to go it alone. We cannot serve two masters. We either depend on Him or ourselves.

"I (the self dominated by sin) have been crucified with Christ; and it is no longer I who live, but Christ lives in me; and the life which I now live in the flesh I (the self that is obsessed with God) live by faith in the Son of God, who loved me, and delivered Himself up for me." Galatians 2:20 (inserts added)

"For God so loved the world that He gave His only begotten Son that whoever believes in Him shall have eternal life." John 3:16

I would paraphrase those two verses this way. The more I depend on God and surrender to His plan the more I have an eternal perspective, love God, the self God is making of me, and other people.

How are we to know which self is in charge?

The answer lies in another question. Are we pursuing true peace or pseudo peace? Each one must answer that question for him or herself.

It is an undeniable truth that for the child of God our deepest need is the love of God spread abroad in our hearts. Once you have walked the Emmaus road and had your heart burn within you, the desire will be satisfied and intensified at the same time. That is another great mystery to full of wonder for us to understand but within the grasps of every honest seeking heart; honest because we acknowledge our utter dependency and seeking because we surrender control of our lives into his loving hands and seek to know His heart's desire for us.

Prayer is the true occupation of every believer.

Our attitude could be of one who is applying for a job. That implies that we must do some specific thing to secure our position. We don't know what exactly that thing is, so we tend to stay focused on what we perceive to be missing from our imaginary resume'.

It is a great grace that the Father God purposed to free us from the fear of failure and the rejection we assume will follow.

Years ago, when I first started getting serious about prayer my concept was of asking God to solve problems. I didn't think of it as worship with the focus on the God who cares for us and uses our problems to lovingly train us. I didn't have a clue as to what I or anyone else really needed. But, I pretty much prayed "answers" to Him anyway. In other words, I thought my role was to come up with several viable solutions to problems, submit them to God and then He could choose the best one. To be sure He does say that, we do not have because we do not ask, but I did not understand how to let Him lead.

Did you know that God laughs?

"He who sits in the heavens laughs, the Lord scoffs at them." Psalm 2:4

He laughs at the kings of the earth that take their stand against the Lord and His anointed.

He didn't laugh at me years ago when I was praying answers to Him. That was all I knew to do, and He was patient with me. He actually did answer many of the prayers I prayed because He knew my heart.

A child will never learn to walk unless he or she takes baby steps. We have all seen a toddler walking successfully as long as an adult is walking behind them. The child's hands are raised to meet the hands of the adult. All goes well until the child's immature legs get tired, they let go and fall to the floor. It takes many tries before they learn how to walk.

Our heavenly Father is like that with us in prayer. He lets us go out ahead just slightly until our spiritual legs get tired. The more we persist in prayer, with hands held high in the universal sign of surrender, the less we rely on ourselves and the more we learn how to walk in the spirit and let Him lead. He becomes to us our Daddy; our Abba Father.

Eventually the toddler in our analogy does walk without the parents help. So, the analogy of the toddler breaks down, in that, we're <u>not</u> required to take off praying on our own. We will only and always learn how to rely on Him to lead.

How do we let Him lead?

"Let this mind be in you which was also in Christ Jesus." Philippians 2:5
The Spirit that lead Jesus will lead you and me.
That is why interceding for others is a divine calling.

Gideon – A Man of Prayer

Judges 6-8

Gideon was not a king like David. But God did call him to lead a nation that was in danger of being overrun by their enemy. He said of himself and his family. "We are the least in Manasseh, and I am youngest in my father's house." Judges 1:15.

He was right in his estimation of himself in that he possessed nothing in himself that was up to the task at hand, but God created him and knew that his divine calling was to save his people.

Gideon was a fearful man, but God saw the raw potential and being the Craftsman He is, God set about to reveal the beautiful image of another man after God's own heart.

He is an example of a man going from one stage of spiritual development to another. Instead of hiding out in an institution he is hiding out at the wine press trying to thresh wheat. He felt safe there. The enemies of his people were "**crouching at their door**" ready to snatch away the precious wheat. Not only does the wheat provide nourishment to the people but without the seed grain there will be no harvest for years to come; famine was inevitable.

A worrier is someone who is tormented with the cares of the world, anxieties and uneasiness. Their peace of mind is destroyed. Fear reigns on the throne of their mind and grumbling follows.

Grumbling expresses unbelief.
Praise, in the face of trouble, expresses faith.

God pronounced him a "Valiant Warrior," before he had done anything to warrant that description; then He proceeded to work with the imperfections that Gideon gave Him to make it a reality.

God does not ask us to do something we can do without Him.
But with the word comes the courage to follow through
to freedom and the power to walk out our calling.

His stage 3 honest skepticism became fertile ground for God to plant spiritual seeds and for those seeds to bring about the privilege of taking action. Eventually Gideon trusted Gods judgment about his calling and then God entrusted him with the desire to fulfill his destiny.

Oswald Chambers said: "It's not so true that "prayer changes things" as that prayer changes *me* and I change things." <u>My Utmost for His Highest</u> August 28th

Things needed to change for the Israelites or all the people would have died.

His people were in serious trouble. There were marauding bands of thieves intent on harming God's people, the Jews, but God had a purpose for allowing the Midianites and the Amalekites to destroy their produce, steal their sheep, oxen and donkeys. The reason they were in this fix was because of their idol worship." They did what was evil in the sight of the Lord." They had rejected Jehovah God and had taken to worshiping Baal.

God did not change the Midianites. But He did change His peoples' disposition (the way they looked at the world) and they changed things as God lead them.

Judges 1:6-34; Judges 7:3

"So Israel was brought very low because of Midian, and the sons of Israel cried to the Lord on account of Midian, then the Lord sent a prophet to the sons of Israel, and he said to them, "Thus says the Lord, the God of Israel, it was I who brought you up from Egypt, and brought up out from the house of slavery. And delivered you from the hands of the Egyptians and from the hands of all your oppressors and dispossessed them before you and gave their land." Verse 7:9

When God said, "It was I who brought you up from Egypt," it is like He was saying remember Me? We have been here before; you rebel, I chasten, you repent, and I deliver. (My paraphrase)

Their older generations had reason to remember and trust in the deliverances of their God.

The prophet of the Lord went on to speak for God saying, "I am the Lord your God; you shall not fear the gods of the Amorites in whose land you live. But you have not obeyed Me." Verse 10

He is saying do not become superstitious about the false gods among you. And I think He is saying, you had better fear Me the God who has every right to judge your behavior.

They lacked awe of His power and reverence for His ability to discipline those He loves.

There are consequences for disobedience, but our God is a God who is willing to forgive and restore if we honestly admit our sin and our desperate need of His guidance.

It was at an extremely low time in Gideon's life that God spoke the words Valiant Warrior. Gideon's response was very human. He said in so many words. "My God, why have you abandoned us?" He was honest in his desperation, but God did not even respond to the grumbling question. God proceeded to say, "Go in your strength and deliver Israel from the hand of Midian, Have I not sent you? (verse 14)

As the dialogue continues Gideon reminds God
of his lowly birth and his immaturity.

Finding things to grumble about is our way of finding justification for our fear.

"But the Lord said to him, Surely I will be with you and you shall defeat Midian as one man." (verse 16)

Before Gideon confronted the flesh and blood enemy of his people, the Midianites, he confronted Baal, the spiritual enemy among them.

After giving offerings to the Lord he experienced several miraculous responses from the Lord that gave him reason to keep moving on down God's chosen path for him. The next step he took was to obey God and pull down the alter of Baal which belonged to his father, he used two bulls to pull down the alter and then he cut down the Asherah that is beside it. Next, he built an alter to the Lord his God on the top of this stronghold. In an orderly manner, he took a second bull, and offered a burnt offering with the wood of the Asherah which he cut down. (My paraphrase)

Gideon had broken down and destroyed the alter of Baal.

It was Gods plan to replace the alter to Baal with an alter to Himself. Gideon repurposed the wood using it to burn the bull offering and, in the process, challenge the false god to defend himself.

Gideon was afraid to do what God told him to do during the day, so he took ten man servants and did it **after dark**. The next morning the men of the village were furious. They wanted to kill Gideon. His father's response was to say, "If he (Baal) is god, let him contend for himself." Verse 31

His birth name had been Gideon; he who breaks, a destroyer. His new name is Jerubbaal which means let Baal contend against him.

"Then all the Midianites and the Amalekites and the sons of the east assembled themselves; and they crossed over and camped in the valley of the Lord." Verse 33

After God's people got their priorities right "things" began to change. The enemy in human form played right into the Lords hands. Notice, it was the valley of the Lord where they chose to assemble. The valley of Megiddo is a historic battleground in the heart of Palestine.

"So, the Spirit of the Lord came upon Gideon; and he blew a trumpet, and the Abiezrites were called together." Verse 34

In this verse, the words "The Spirit of the Lord came upon Gideon" literally means that he was clothed by the Spirit. I wonder if Gideon felt like he was wrapped in a velvet blanket.

Gideon sent messages to many other oppressed people and they joined him.

But Gideon was not absolutely sure that all this was really God's plan. He proceeded to pray "answers" to God in the form of a test. He put fleece out to collect dew and then the next **night** he put one out to repel the dew that fell from the sky in the early mornings. God was patient with him. He had a purpose for Gideon's life that Gideon did not realize. Even when he put out fleece and asked God to verify the assignment God did not reprimand or chasten him. In fact, He accommodated Gideon's request and rewarded his **stepping out** with the response Gideon had asked for.

Now God takes the lead and announces the battle plan. He told Gideon that he had too many men. God had taken a sovereign census and determined that the people were in danger of becoming self-assured by a victory with so many men.

First, He said to the men, "Whoever is afraid and trembling, let him return and depart from Mount Gilead." Twenty-two thousand men had come but only then thousand remained. Judges 7:3 (my paraphrase)

Then, God chose to reduce the number to only 300, lest the people become proud and boastful. The method God chose was amazing. Out of the 10,000 men; 9,700 lapped the drinking water with their tongue. This revealed their tendency to ignore their surroundings. They did not remain alert. Those who put their hand in the water and then brought the water to their mouth showed attentiveness and vigilance.

God could see that Gideon was still fearful and needed more reassurance.

Again, **after dark**, Gideon did something that God allowed in order to prove His sovereign plan was in fact the plan of the age to deliver His people. Gideon snuck down to the enemy camp where he over- heard a man recount a dream. His dream pronounced that God had given Midian and all the camp into Gideon's hand.

That was exactly what he needed to hear.
He had difficulty envisioning himself the way God saw him.
God changed Gideon's name from Fearful Worrier to Valiant Warrior.

So, you ask what is the difference between Gideon's fearfulness and the fearful thousands? I don't know for sure, but I believe it has everything to do with God's personal plan for each of them. He will give us grace for the things He calls us to do but not for the things He calls someone else to do. We can rest assured in the fact that He will send exactly the problems we need to press us into Himself. And He will send us home if we are afraid that God will not do what He said He would do. He also cannot use us if we are trying to be courageous in our own strength or fill a job description that He did not design for us. And of course, He sees the big picture and knows that it was for the benefit of the people to recognize that only the true God could bring about victory in this miraculous way and with so few men.

One more difference of note between Gideon and the fearful thousands; Gideon prayed and kept praying. He sought the Lord and was rewarded for it.

There is a battle raging inside us. Which self will we serve? And there is the battle outside us. Will we enter in the spiritual battle or accept the path-of-least-resistance? Whether the battle is within us or outside us the answer is to submit to God and resist the Devil.

Gideon had rejected the self that sin had made of him and he respected the self God was making. It required a lot of dialogue, but he did not give up on the process or give in to the emotion of fear that plagued him. God knew his weaknesses and used them for His glory.

GLORY TO THE MASTER AND GLORY TO THE MASTERED ONE

The mighty 300 were successful in the plan God had for them. They divided into groups of 100 and proceeded to approach the outskirts of the enemy camp at about **10 o'clock at night**. They blew trumpets, broke pitchers, that had concealed lit torches. At the same time, they said," A sword for the Lord and for Gideon." Verse 20

The noise and the sudden light made visible by the broken pitchers caused the whole enemy army to flee as if their lives were in danger. There remained no doubt in the mind of God's people who was the true God. And there remained no doubt that His plan was for their good; to give them a future and a hope.

Gideon stepped up to God's challenge. He stepped out in faith and gave the younger generation another reason to believe in the mighty hand of God and His willingness to save the repentant. Remember the actions that set this deliverance in motion were the PRAYERS of the people and the PRAYERS of their leader.

The sons of Israel cried to God from a place deeper and lower;
A place where He could be found.
They cried to the Lord because of their flesh
and blood enemy, the Midianites.

THE TRUE BATTLE

The true battle is not against flesh and blood, but it is against powers and principalities in heavenly places." (my paraphrase) Ephesians 6:12

Jeremiah wept about the rebellion of the people of his day that where worshiping false gods and the inevitable consequences that would follow.

Jesus wept at the grave of Lazarus. His tears revealed His heart for people. He wept over the things that really mattered.

"To the degree that you share the sufferings of Christ, keep on rejoicing so that also at the revelation of His glory, you may rejoice with exaltation. If you are reviled for the name of Christ, you are blessed, because the Spirit of Glory rests upon you." 1 Peter 4:13-14

PRAYER IS WARFARE

Gideon was clothed in God's righteousness and empowered by His Spirit. He submitted to God and resisted the enemy of our souls. God's desire was to restore the people to relationship but only on His terms.

THE ARMOR OF THE LORD

Ephesians 6:10-18

We have established that order is very important to God. With that in mind let us examine the armor of the God. We are blessed to have the New Testament description of God's armor to enrich and bless us. If we are faithful even in the little things, He will entrust us with true spiritual riches.

"Finally, be strong in the Lord and in the strength of His might. Put on the full armor of God, that you may be able to stand firm against the schemes of the Devil. For our struggle is not against flesh and blood, but against the rulers, against the powers, against the world forces of this darkness, against the spiritual forces of wickedness in the heavenly places. Therefore, take up the full armor of God, that you may be able to resist in the evil day, and having done everything to stand firm. Stand firm therefore,"

"HAVING GIRDED YOUR LOINS WITH <u>TRUTH</u>"

Paul did not list the armor from head to foot. He began with the loins. Several times in the Bible the abdomen is referred to in relation to emotions of the human spirit. Gird means to wrap or bind which is an action taken on our part. Satan knows well if he can stir up the emotions that often lie to us about God, he has a foothold in our lives. Remember we are bound to that which we give ourselves. Paul said he was a bond-servant of Christ. That literally means he was willing to be a slave; which comes from the word "to bind." When we voluntarily bind ourselves to Christ, we give up our rights to ourselves relinquishing our claim to ourselves and have no will of our own. This decision, like love, is an act of our will submitted to God; emotions will follow. If our emotions do lead us, we will be perpetually unstable.

It is easy to see why God's truth His priority is #1 for us.

It is worthy to note that in Bible times men wore loose fitting robes and the only time they pulled up their clothing and secured it to their abdomen was to go into battle.

"HAVING PUT ON THE BREASTPLATE OF <u>RIGHTEOUSNESS</u>." **Verse 14b**

Next comes the breastplate of righteousness that protects the vital organs of the heart and lungs. If the physical heart represents the spiritual heart it would serve us well to remember these words spoken by Jeremiah, "The heart is deceitful above all things, and it is exceedingly perverse and corrupt and severely, mortally sick! Who can know it (perceive, understand, be acquainted with his own heart and mind?" Jeremiah 17:9 The Amplified Bible. All the more reason for the righteousness of Jesus Christ to cover the heart.

"AND HAVING SHOD YOUR FEET WITH THE PREPARATION OF THE GOSPEL OF <u>PEACE</u>." **Verse 15**

The third part of the armor is protection for the part of the body that symbolizes mobility. If we are to grow in our relationship with our Savior we can't be looking down at our feet; that is, looking out for ourselves. The stones on the path mustn't be allowed to disturb our peace. There is no need to focus on them when the sandals are prepared to give us the peace that passes all understanding. The gospel is the good news that Jesus Christ is risen from the dead and he is Lord!

"IN ADDITION TO ALL, TAKING UP THE SHIELD OF <u>FAITH</u> WITH WHICH YOU WILL BE ABLE TO EXTINGUISH ALL THE FLAMING MISSILES OF THE EVIL ONE." **Verse 16**

The words "in addition to all" make it very clear that we are to keep this teaching in its proper order. True faith in the living God must be grounded on His truth, His righteousness and His peace. Some people seem to have faith in faith. That is to say, their focus is on themselves and the knowledge they have accumulated. The enemy will see that self-assured "pseudo faith" as a bullseye target.

"AND TAKE THE HELMET OF <u>SALVATION</u>, AND THE SWORD OF THE SPIRIT, WHICH IS <u>THE WORD OF GOD</u>." **Verse 17**

I think it is very interesting that the helmet of salvation and the sword of the Spirit are mentioned last. Perhaps the helmet is last because the choice of whether to become a soldier and prayer warrior is a mental decision. All the more reason to embrace the truth of 1 Peter 1:13; "Gird your minds for action, keep sober in spirit, fix your hope completely on the grace to be brought to you at the revelation of Jesus Christ."

Could it be that the sword of the Spirit which is the Word of God is the very last part of the armor because <u>God will have the last word?</u>

The sword is the only offensive weapon. So, how do we go on the offensive?

We go on the offensive when we remember that we are going to focus on someone or something. Why not make the Lord our priority #1? **His written word** is the light for our pathway and living in His **experienced presence** is the true delight of our new self; the self He is making of us.

A PRAYER THAT CLOTHS US IN HIS ARMOR

I declare and proclaim that I take my place in Your
cross, Your death, and Your resurrection.
I bring myself under your rule; Jesus Christ my Lord.
I die to my sin and I claim the power You so freely give.
In that power, I acknowledge that I live in a world that is at war and
I wield the Spirit's sword to cut off attacks of the enemy.
I sever any agreements I have wittingly or
unwittingly made with the enemy.
Restore me Lord. Give me strength to live and fight another day.
I embrace Your restoration and embrace Your promise that,
"No weapon formed against me will prosper." Is 54:17

Prosper defined: to go forward, increase, thrive, gain or succeed

"So shall my word be that goes out from my mouth; it shall not return empty, but it shall accomplish that which I purpose, and shall succeed . . . Isaiah 55:11 ESC

My paraphrase of the two verses above: No plot, ploy or plan of the enemy will stop us from moving forward toward our goal of pressing on in Christ Jesus. In fact, as he tries to destroy our faith God will always use the process to press us into Himself and He will prove that all these things work for our good. His purposes will increase, thrive and succeed.

A PRAYER OF PRAISE AND GRATITUDE

We praise and honor You Lord.
You are always looking out for us in ways we
only see dimly in this fallen world.
When we see You in heaven we will be like You and
then all these things will be added to our
awareness,
For now, we stand firm and live by faith.
We embrace our divine calling to pray intercessory prayers for others.
We express our gratitude with an honest seeking heart! AMEN

"Lay aside the old self, which is being corrupted in accordance with the lusts of deceit, and that you be renewed in the spirit of your mind, and put on the new self, which in the likeness of God has been created in righteousness and holiness of the truth." Ephesians 4:24

"With all prayer and petition pray at all times in the Spirit, and with this in view, <u>be on the alert with all</u> <u>perseverance and petition for all the saints</u>." **Verse 18**

"Take up the full armor of God, that you may be able to resist in the evil day, and having done everything, to stand firm. Stand firm" Ephesians 6:13,14a

The mighty 300 warriors were alert, they persevered even when it didn't look like the battle plan could possibly work. Their eyes were not looking down. Their feet were shod with the good news that with God all things are possible (Matthew 19:26) even though, humanly speaking, the odds were against them.

If our focus is on God then we can say with confidence; "If God is for us, who is against us?" Romans 8:31b

No self-protection allowed; pain will come and go
but the word of the Lord will endure forever.
In our everyday life, what does that look like?

"As odd or nearly impossible as it may seem, we are to welcome our times of trouble as we would greet a friend who has been gone a long time. We are to meet trials with joy (James 1:2) and rejoice when suffering comes (Romans 5:3). Why? Because suffering sets into motion our will to find meaning; it compels us to honestly assess the facts of our lives and begin to order truth into a framework that has personal meaning to us. We cannot have a sense of purpose or deep understanding of what we are created for unless we encounter the kind of pain that compels us to rise above the daily domain and recollect who we are. Pain enables us to discover ourselves." Dan B. Allender <u>The Healing Path</u> pg. 37

"Consider it all joy, my brethren, when you encounter various trials, knowing that the testing of your faith produces endurance." James 1:2-3

Endurance defined: patience, willingness to wait for the Lord's perfect timing

Paul said that he rejoiced in tribulations because he knew that times of trouble bring about perseverance. Romans 5:3 (My paraphrase)

Perseverance defined: the will to keep going on down the road with the Lord even when the going gets tough

Pressed Into God for Impossible Things

There are those times when the pressure is so intense that we do find it impossible to think in terms of the truth encapsulated by Dan Allender. Pressure can strain our minds to the point that hearing God and responding to Him is beyond our human abilities to formulate prayer. It may feel like He is far away, but it is then that the precious Holy Spirit intercedes for us with groanings too **deep** for words. He sees our heart and knows that if we could pray . . . we would. We can't. So, He does. We are never alone. Those precious "collectable" stones are being stored away as stones of remembrance. When the pressure seems like more than we can stand we have even more reason to believe in our Lord's mighty hand of deliverance; gratitude follows as sure as the sun rises in the east.

"This I recall to my mind; therefore I have **hope**. The Lord's loving kindnesses indeed never cease, for His compassions never fail. They are new every morning; great is His faithfulness. The Lord is my portion, says my soul, therefore I have hope in Him. The Lord is good to those who wait for Him, **to the person who seeks Him**. "Lamentations 3:21-25

Hope defined: comfort, expectation, confidence, trust

So, if speaking audible words is not the requirement for intimacy with our Lord; what is required?

We must accept that the situation we are in is allowed by God. He either prescribed it by His sovereign will or He will redeem our wanderings; either way He is on our side. The intensity will pass. Moments of peace will give way to minutes, hours and days. The light of His presence begins to illumine the tunnel we feel like we are in and His love revealed shines on our path again. Panic gives way to gratitude. Peace resumes (picks up where it left off) and we will never quite be the same.

We recollect who we are; One Who Seeks His Face.

Michael Wells said, "In His presence and by His power, the ten commandments become the ten promises; that we will not commit those sins."

So even when we read a list of requirements in the bible we are not overwhelmed. We even learn to love His statutes.

"O how I love Thy law! It is my meditation all the day." Psalm 119:97

"I will meditate on Thy precepts, and regard Thy ways. I shall delight in Thy statues; I shall not neglect Thy word." Psalm 119:15-16

GOD'S REQUIREMENTS

"What does our God require of us?" Do justice, love kindness and walk humbly with our God." Micah 6:8

"Do justice"

"Love does not rejoice in unrighteousness but rejoices with the truth." 1 Corinthians 13:6

"Love kindness"

"Love is patient, love is kind and is not jealous, love
does not brag and is not arrogant." 1 Cor 13:4

"Walk humbly with our God."

"Love does not act unbecomingly; it does not seek its own, is not
provoked, does not take into account a wrong suffered." 1 Cor. 13:5

"<u>Love never fails</u>." 1 Cor 13:8a

"But now abide faith, hope, love, these three; but
the greatest is LOVE." 1 Cor. 13:13

God doesn't call the qualified. He qualifies the called.
Author unknown

Gideon prayed childlike prayers. God heard him and met him right
where he was. He gets down on His knees among us today when we
acknowledge our need for guidance. He says to us; "This is the way, walk
in it."

The Israelites honestly assessed the facts and began to order truth into
a framework that had meaning to them. Prayer, that two way conversation,
gave release to their deep understanding of the purpose to which they had
been called. Prayer gave them motivation to proceed on down the road He
had called them to travel. They were created to live at that exact time in
history and it was the pain of their lives that compelled them to pray God
inspired prayers. Hope<u>ful</u>ness displaced hope<u>less</u>ness and God received the
glory and praise He had deserved all along.

I like to think of Dan Allender's treatise on problems as wisdom
for getting in touch with Reality and the power God gives us to "rise to
the occasion." The praying people of Gideon's day rose to the occasion,
prayed God inspired prayers that released the power of God to deliver their
countrymen from the hands of the enemy. It is said that in any war; for
every soldier in the front lines there are many support personnel. Those

who prayed were soldiers in God's army just as much as the 300 who marched with Gideon.

"Prayer is not preparation for the work. Prayer is the work to which we are called, and everybody is commanded to pray. Each of us has a place in the battle where we stand in the gap. If we don't stand in our particular place the enemy will come in like a flood. Please Lord help us to not be AWOL. Help us to report to duty with our armor on ready for battle." Blessing Your Spirit by Sylvia Gunter and Arthur Burk

"I sought for a man among them, that should make up the hedge, and stand in the gap before me for the land." Ezekiel 22:30

A WARRIORS PRAYER

Lord, show us Your strategies.

Reveal the part of Your plan that involves us.

And help us rise to the occasion.

Oh God, I praise You and bow to Your Sovereignty. You use the darkness to bring about Your will. The enemy is confounded and dispatched as we answer, "Yes Lord" to Your calling. May the Light of Your presence be so precious to us that the thought of sin allowing distance between us for even a moment becomes reason to cry out, "Abba Father." Amen and Amen

CHAPTER 16

THE STRAIGHT AND NARROW WAY

"Enter by the narrow gate; for the gate is wide, and the way is broad that leads to destruction and many are those who enter by it. For the gate is small and the way is narrow that leads to life and few are those who find it." Matthew 7:13-14

I think we have established that the One and only true God of the Bible is loving, kind, patient and determined to grow us up in our spirit and to mold us into His image.

That is why God presents us with His armor. He knows we need it. He gives us instructions on how to apply the armor and opportunities to experience wielding the sword.

Have you ever had a brief encounter with someone you had never met before, but you recognize the Lord's presence dwelling within them? There's a connection that is very difficult to describe in words. It's as though words flow easily without effort. As far as brief encounters are concerned all is well, but we mustn't be naive. Everyone we encounter will not be worthy of our trust. The Bible tells us to test the spirits. Job did just that when his "friends" where not speaking for God. They were speaking for the enemy of our souls. He refused to be intimidated into agreeing with their opinion of him.

Perhaps it is more true than we want to admit that going into spiritual battle seems overwhelming and scary. The enemy uses those emotions to distract us, keep us disengaged, inattentive, and disinterested. He wants us to be distracted and preoccupied with other issues. His goal is to outmaneuver us and condition us to ignore his lies and his attacks. The evil Jezebel spirit is one of intimidation. If we don't go to battle, fear and hopelessness will rule the person under attack.

Could we harbor a hidden fear that if we take a stand against the enemy, he will redouble his efforts against us?

What I just described is intimidation on his side
and superstitious fear on our side.
Our best military maneuver is to stay on the straight and narrow.
Even if he does attack because of our efforts remember
the winner of the wrestling match is our God.
He will fight our battles for us. He will do the part that only He can do.
"Trust in the Lord with all your heart, and do not lean on
your own understanding. In all your ways acknowledge Him,
and He will make your paths **straight**." Proverbs 3:5-6
Jesus is the Gate, the Way and the Rock
Holy Spirit is our Guide

We need a travel guide. Jesus told us in John 16:13 that when the Spirit of truth comes. He will guide us into all truth.

Our eternal salvation is as easy as a genuine prayer of repentance and acceptance of the gift of salvation Jesus so freely offers. But a life typified by the narrow way will not be easy. If it was easy Paul would not have said, "We exalt in our tribulations, knowing that tribulation brings about perseverance; and perseverance proven character, and proven character hope; and hope does not disappoint, because the love of God has been poured out with in our hearts through the Holy Spirit who was given to us." Romans 5:3-5

That sounds like the path of "most resistance" to the world, the flesh and the devil. But make no mistake, for the child of God, the narrow way is the most exciting and fulfilling way of life!

The Bible says that few will enter by the narrow gate. So, it stands to reason that religious movements cannot tout their legitimacy because of large numbers. "Many people" does not equal conformation of truth any more than "many words" constitute real prayer.

If both gates had a sign the wide gate sign would read, "All Paths Lead to Heaven - Everyone Enter Here." If you embrace a world philosophy in keeping with any set of rules that promotes the idea that you can accumulate a reservoir of favor that God will accept; you have believed a lie. That false doctrine produces pride and contradicts everything the Bible says about redemption and reconciliation. This is the lie of every false religion. It is a perfect example of self-styled "worship activities" of which the Bible has no description. God will reject this journey to the far country.

> They accumulate false favor from like-minded
> people. Their reward will be in this life only.
> This could be described as the path of "least resistance."

He also said, "We are no longer children, tossed here and there by waves, and carried about by craftiness in deceitful scheming." Ephesians 4:14

Any doctrine that promises to give its followers chills, thrills, health, and wealth is to be rejected. It is not biblical and many people who say "Lord, Lord" will find out after it's too late that they have been on the broad path to destruction. It's alluring to want all our problems solved in an exciting way. Listen to the apostle Matthew.

"Beware of the false prophets, who come to you in sheep's clothing, but inwardly are ravenous wolves. You will know them by their fruits. Grapes are not gathered from thorn bushes, nor figs from thistles, are they?" So then, you will know them by their fruits. Not everyone who says to Me, Lord, Lord will enter the kingdom of heaven; but he who does the will of My Father who is in heaven. Many will say to Me on that day, Lord, Lord did we not prophecy in Your name, and in Your name cast out demons, and in Your name perform many miracles? And then I will declare to them, "I never knew you; DEPART FROM ME, YOU WHO PRACTICE LAWLESSNESS." Matthew 7:15-16,20-23 (emphases added)

Remember, in the previous chapter Oswald Chambers cautioned us about entering random gateways to spiritually. God places barriers for our benefit. When He says, "Not that way" He means it.

163

If there was a sign above the small gate it would read;" Only Forgiven Sinners Enter Heaven Here."

Our sins are imputed or placed on Jesus. His
righteousness is imparted to us.

Imputed defined: Even though Jesus was the sinless Son of God He died for us. Our sin was placed on Him and Jesus died to wipe away the death sentence that was passed down to us through Adam and Eve. God told them not to eat of the tree of the knowledge of good and evil or they would surely die. Jesus died willingly to pay the price that a righteous God requires.

Imparted righteousness defined: Holy Spirit works **in the Christian** to enable and empower the process of sanctification that sets us apart for service. The righteousness of Jesus Christ has been credited to the Christian. Our commuted "death sentence" enables the believer to be justified in the Fathers eyes. He treats us as if, through faith in Jesus, His righteousness is our own.

For unbelievers the difference between the two
gates is eternal life or eternal death.
We believers in Jesus accumulate rewards in heaven that last forever.

It helps to examine our spiritual focus.

On the straight and narrow way, we will find ourselves between the Rock and many hard places. Jesus is the Rock, and our problems are those hard places. We must decide if we will have our eyes focused on Him or them.

Do we have our eyes fixed on the Author and Finisher of our faith or are we focusing on our problems so intensely that Jesus' presence seems blurred and distant? It is an act of the will to submit to God by staying ever mindful of Him. Sometimes a word picture helps us do that.

I like to think about a tight rope walker. You know what I mean. There are those people who manage to stay upright and walk on a very narrow band. It's clearly not a normal activity. There must be something inside them that motivates them to tackle a task that seems foreign to most of us. This is where the human bodies connective tissue comes in handy. Positioning, balance, and coordination help with stability. They look down at their feet long enough to position themselves on the rope. Then the walker looks up to focus their eyes on a point ahead. That focus requires concentration. Let's think of the tight rope as the "straight and narrow way," or in other words "Gods will." The focal point is Jesus Christ. Think of the height as the dangerous world that tempts us and our flesh as the gravitational pull downward. And never forget Holy Spirit is our stability. He is our counterbalance and the tissue that connects us to the Father.

There is a saying that encourages us to trust our strong-willed independent attitudes. It goes like this:

"Where there's a will, there's a way."
I would rather say, "Where's there's God's will, there's God's way."

Our God promises us that when we keep our eyes on Him, acknowledge Him in all our ways, do not lean on our own understanding, He will make our paths straight to and through the narrow gate.

Another example of an exceptional ability to stay balanced when the going gets tough is the majestic deer that is able to conquer fear, walk a slippery slope and function with precision and confidence.

"For who is God, but the Lord? And who is a rock, except our God? The God who girds me with strength and makes my way blameless? He makes my feet like hinds' feet and sets me upon my high places. He trains my hands for battle, so that my arms can bend a bow of bronze." Psalm 18:31-34

He sets us upon our high places; the upward call of Christ Jesus and He gives us stability. He enlists us in His service, takes care of us and prepares us for skirmishes that are inevitable. He keeps us sure-footed in our faith even when facing a life of challenges.

In reality, we know that we will fall from time to time. This is where the analogy ends. Instead of hitting the floor or bouncing in a net like a person falling from a tight rope or sliding down the mountain to our death, we fall into the arms of a loving Father who encourages us to learn of Him, and fills our minds with gratitude for His protection and His patience.

If we resist His leading spiritual paralysis can set in and He will have to break us of our stubbornness.

> What we need is the positioning that comes to
> us from partnership with our Lord.

Sometimes course corrections are needed. If you are sitting by the side of the road it will not happen. We must stay moving toward our destiny while staying in a spiritual place that recognizes God's leading.

Paul said, "Brethren, I do not regard myself as having laid hold of it yet; but one thing I do: forgetting what lies behind and reaching forward to what lies ahead, I press on toward the goal for the prize of the upward call of God in Christ Jesus. " Philippians 3:13-14

> Remember this; it is in Him we live and
> move . . . (Acts 17:28 my paraphrase)

When we choose to walk the narrow way our mind often thinks of living a life of legalistic restricted behaviors. Unless God places you in a situation like Jerimiah; rules only feed a need we have boundaries that serve to keep God as far away as possible. God wants us to die to ourselves, submit to Him first, and then move on to intercessory prayer. He wants us to pour out our lives for others and pray prayers that flow from a heart overflowing with Gods' love.

I want to share with you a few prayer techniques that help me get moving on the straight and narrow way. The first one will sound like a very elementary activity. It is for the purpose of presenting the issues of my life to God.

Here goes. I get a blank sheet of copy paper. The first thing I do is draw an empty shape like a circle, a heart shape, a star of David in the center of the page or the outline of a cross at the top of a page leaving space for prayer issues at the foot of the cross. The empty symbol is for the purpose of filling that space with one of the many names of God. Chapter nine pages 74-75 has a list of Gods character traits and His attributes. Then I let God lead me as I write out prayer issues randomly around the center symbol or at the foot of the cross symbol. I do not try to prioritize them. And I make no requests.

But I do draw a line from each issue toward God's name. This is my way of <u>proclaiming</u> God as the supreme Ruler of the universe and <u>invoking</u> His Spirit to rule and reign over the time we spend together. Focusing on the name of God establishes myself as helpless to fix anything and establishes God as the only One who is able to bring deliverance. I cannot explain to you what a blessing it is to get my burdens out of my mind and on paper. No complaining! I am presenting them to God. In effect I am saying, "What are the burdens of Your heart Lord?" Then I thank Him for listening to me. Prayer requests often follow this exercise.

Proclaiming defined: to announce and declare the truth of Gods Sovereignty

Invoking defined: an earnest appeal to God as the ultimate authority, a call to Him in prayer for inspiration

Inspiration defined: when God breaths life into human thoughts

I've found that when I write out praises, thanks and requests on another sheet of paper it helps me stay focused. I am more likely to be engaged, attentive, and interested in Gods' solutions to those problems. I don't try to compose a formal prayer. I just jot down my thoughts. If my mind wanders, I can read what I have written and start where I left off. I get to share the kind of give and take conversation that gives joy to our Lord. Just think of it, the God of the universe wants to converse with me and you. Before the sinful fall of mankind, He walked with them in the garden. For now, our conversation has interruptions. In heaven it will be like it was in the garden before the fall; only better.

It is worthy to note Jesus' advice to His disciples. First, He teaches them how NOT to pray.

"When you are praying do not use meaningless repetition as the Gentiles do, for they suppose that they will be heard for their many words, "therefore do not be like them; for your <u>Father knows what you need before you ask Him.</u>" Matthew 6:7-8 (emphases added)

Then Jesus proceeds to give them a model for prayer. It starts with adoration for God. Next, it declares God as the ruler of His Kingdom in heaven and on earth. Without stating it implicitly we know that we are His subjects in the Kingdom. On that basis he urges us to make requests that are in keeping with His kingdom priorities, and it ends with words of praise and adoration.

The Lord's Prayer - Matthew 6:9-13

"Pray, then, in this way: Our father who art
in heaven, hallowed be thy name.
Thy kingdom come. Thy will be done, on earth as it is in heaven.
Give us this day our daily bread.
And forgive us our debits, as we also have forgiven our debtors.
And do not lead us into temptation, but deliver us from evil.
For thine is the kingdom, and the power, and the glory, forever. Amen"

Jesus has intrinsic glory that exists whether we acknowledge it or not. When we give Him glory, we are not adding to His glory. We are acknowledging the truth and aligning ourselves with Him. We are stating that which is obviously true.

John 14:13 tells us some very important information. Jesus said, "Whatever you ask in My name, that will I do, that the Father may be glorified in the Son. If you ask Me anything in My name, I will do it."

Since He knows what we need before we ask, it stands to reason that Spirit prompted prayers are those that are not planned out but flow from asking in Jesus name.

So, what does the term "in Jesus name" mean? I think it is a type of prayer that is representative of His character and focused on His will. They are prayers that address the Father through the Son asking for the things Christ would want to happen.

Jesus name, in Hebrew, literally means salvation. As our Savior He promises us many things along the narrow way.

Prayer is God's promise turned into petition.
We should claim God's promises in all the areas of our lives.
God bases His promises on the condition of prayer
because it shows that we want what God wants.
As we ask, seek and knock our desires become
aligned with Him and miraculously
the process of prayer transforms us.
It changes us from "One Who Wants Our Own Way" to
"One Who Delights in His Will and His Way."
After God changes us then and only then can we change things.

When I write out my prayers my goal is not MANY WORDS. Repetition may be a result of trying to pray long prayers instead of meaningful prayers. To put it simply, we run out of words to say. I will share with you another prayer method that gets my mind engaged and focused.

"I COME . . ."

The first verse of the old hymn "Just as I Am" reminds me that I am acceptable just as I am because Jesus died for my sin. He is the Lamb that was slain, and He requests my presence. I have a choice. I can come to Him or go my own way.

Just as I am, without one plea, But that Thy blood was shed for me.
And that Thou bidd'st me come to Thee, O
Lamb of God, I come! I Come!

I am very familiar with the tune. Sometimes I hum the whole first verse, but I almost always sing the lilting tune of the last four notes and recite the last four words, I come . . .I come . . .

Another hymn that comes to mind is "Jesus is Calling." The first verse begins like this:

Jesus is tenderly calling me home – calling today.

HOME IS PRAYER FOR NOW – HEAVEN IS OUR HOME FOR ETERNITY

Home is a place to rest. A place to rise up with energy and purpose. A place where we can be ourselves; no pretense needed.

Then, a simple slogan I love to repeat is this: I listen – You say – I pray

By this time, I'm usually ready to proceed writing and praying. The words of these hymns set to music have a profound effect on my spirit and open my heart to seek Him. It is here in this quiet place near to the heart of God where I find peace. I can believe that He will always lead me to pray prayers that are on His heart and that those prayers bear the name of the Creator. I will meditate on His word. I will dwell on His sovereignty, soak up the rays of His presence and I will wait for Him to lead me. I call this process "centering down."

I am not suggesting that everyone should use my personal methods of prayer that I describe. If God leads you to pray using these prayer methods, I hope they will bless you. But He may want to express Himself through you in ways that are very special and unique, which leads me to a very important question. How can you be certain that the ideas that come to your mind are from God? There are only three sources of inspiration.

There is our flesh, our foe and our Father. Our flesh wants to indulge us. The enemy of our soul wants to undo us. God wants to subdue and renew us.

God wants to bless us, but He has to conquer us first.
Then and only then do we have the ammunition to
conquer the world, the flesh, and the devil.
Romans 8:37 "But in all these things we overwhelmingly
conquer through Him who loved us."

I don't mean to imply that I have this all figured out; rather, I submit to you that God is always reaching out to us. Often there are barriers to worship. As child of God those barriers are on our side. I will share with you some of the things I have learned along my way.

There are thoughts that come to mind that are not personal reflection. So, back to the question, "How do we know that an idea is from God?"

First and foremost, an idea or an impression will agree with the Bible. God will never contradict Himself nor will He allow anything to be added to or taken away from the written word. That is one reason why reading the Bible is so important. The way George Mueller read the Bible allows God to give us information while practicing His presence. George said the first great and primary business each day was to get his inner man nourished. He embraced his anointing.

Anointing defined: It is the promise of illumination from the Holy Spirit which leads us to a true understanding of the Bible and God.

We do not have to be a renowned theologian like A.W. Tozer or a spiritual giant like George Mueller. The anointing is available to every believer.

John 16:13-15 "But when He, the Spirit of truth, comes, He will guide you into all the truth; for He will not speak on His own initiative, but whatever He hears, He will speak; and He will disclose to you what is to come."

He will shine His light and illuminate the narrow way before us.

Second, if a thought doesn't mold us to His image it's not from God. If it is self-serving and full of selfish ambition, we can be assured that God is not in it. The love of God poured out in our hearts will inspire us to submit to Gods' will done Gods' way. Let me be very clear, self-interest and self-responsibility are not sin. God does not want us to expect someone to take care of us.

But, if we harbor angry thoughts the stress of those thoughts can make it very difficult to hear His still small voice. They will impede our ability to know if a thought is from God or not.

"Let all bitterness and wrath and anger and clamor and slander be put away from you, along with all malice. And be kind to one another, tenderhearted, forgiving each other, just as God in Christ also has forgiven you." Ephesians 4:31 (paraphrase)

Malice defined- the desire to get even with someone

"Never pay back evil for evil to anyone." God said; "Vengeance is mine, I will repay." Romans 12:17a19b

In His sovereignty, God knows everything. But as Michael Wells put it, "In every situation there are many facts we have no way of knowing."

Sometimes I think we "pray" as a way of justifying a bad attitude; one that is judgmental, critical, harsh, accusing and unforgiving. It is very easy to be critical. It's not so easy to be forgiving and sincerely impartial. Before we can pray for others, we have to get the beam out of our own eye. (paraphrase of Matthew 7:4-5) Then and only then can we see clearly to pray for them.

If these feelings prevail, we might as well be honest and admit it to Him. He already knows anyway. A simple repentant prayer will bring freedom to pray as He intended. If we don't repent these feelings will wear us down and wear us out.

Proverbs 28: 13 "He who conceals his transgressions will not prosper. But he who confesses and forsakes them will find compassion."

This does not mean that we have to clean up our act before we come to Him. The exact opposite is true. We are to bring our broken heart wounded by other people's actions, and we admit that it just might be God we are angry with.

Just go to Him with your pain. No one has suffered more than Jesus suffered on our behalf. He can identify with our pain and He will never reject an honest seeking heart.

Remember, He is always with us. We are never alone. He takes away nothing that does not already belong to Him. We have no reason to complain, fret or rage. After all, we do not deserve His gifts. So, in affliction we praise Him.

People are different and there are different types of forgiveness. The forgiveness journey is difficult for everyone. Sometimes the process means complete restoration of a relationship. Other times healthy boundaries stay in place. It is a divine process that requires the power of God and the realization that forgiveness is not about the other person admitting their guilt. Nor is it trying to tell yourself "it didn't matter". Forgiveness is the release of that person to God and saying; "God You deal with them." God's order is dependance on Him and surrender to his will. Feelings will follow. It helps to remember that God has forgiven us all so much we have an obligation to forgive other people.

Furthermore, God does not ask us to do anything we can do on our own. With the command to forgive comes the God given power to follow through to a place of peace. The divine process comes from within us where He resides, and the process will reveal things about us that needed mending anyway. Friends may help but when memories trigger a mental replay of the incident or incidences the choice is ours. We either accept the invitation to "Learn from Him because He is gentle and humble, and FIND REST FOR YOUR SOULS" or we reject His **gift** of forgiveness". (Matthew 11:29 paraphrased)

GOING ON THE OFFENSIVE

"WRITE – READ - DESTROY"

"Take up the helmet of salvation and the <u>sword of the Spirit</u>, which is the word of God." Ephesians 6:17

To "take up" something describes an action. Our part is to obey His command to put on the whole armor. God will do the miraculous.

The helmet of salvation does many things for us. One of which is to protect our thoughts. The word of God is the only offensive weapon mentioned.

One way to take action and suspend spiritual paralysis is to get the resentment out of your mind and on to a sheet of paper. The action needs to be memorable enough to serve as a purging project. It has the potential to remove the seeds of resentment that the enemy uses as ammunition to keep healing from happening. One time I was poised to Write Read and Destroy but the Lord reminded me of a time when I had done something similar to the offence I was about to record. I instantly felt no need to proceed. So, don't be surprised if God uses the process in any way He chooses.

First, submit to God by praying God's blessing and guidance over your time together. Next, briefly write out the offence, read through it and tear up the paper it is written on. Typing it out on the computer and hitting delete is not memorable enough to be helpful when sometime later your mind starts to ruminate, and it will, about the incident. When the enemy reminds you of that incident the resistance to his prompting begins by choosing to bring back to your mind the process of writing, reading and destroying. The process ends with a resolve to let go and let God have His way. You can stand in the belief that the enemy will flee from you. As the process proceeds you may remember more details and feel the need repeat writing reading and destroying again but the idea is to move on past the offence; not to rehash it over and over.

Prayerfully writing out the offence unlocks the memory. Reading through it walks you out through that door and destroying the sheet slams shut the prison door behind you. Then you are free to stand, walk and move on with your life.

"Take up the full armor of God, that you may be able to resist in the evil day and having done everything to stand firm. Stand firm. Ephesians 6:13

"Submit therefore to God. Resist the devil and he will flee from you." James 4:7

"Take up the helmet of salvation and the sword of the Spirit which is the word of God." Ephesians 6:17

Forgiving Other People is a Gift from God.

"Every good and perfect gift is coming down from the Father of heavenly lights, who does not change like shifting shadows." James 1:17

He is the Lamb that was slain,
Only He is worthy to say;
"Father forgive them, they don't know what they are doing."
Forgiveness is a choice not a feeling.
He will forgive **through** you.
God told Jerimiah to extract the precious from the worthless.
Hatred is worthless. Forgiveness is priceless.

Relationships with other believers are crucial to our spiritual growth and coping with life's stresses and problems. As I have said before, God is less concerned with our comfort and more concerned with our maturity. Willingness to listen to one another helps us grow up in the Lord. But the gate is not wide enough for a group. Entering through that gate is not a group event.

Another way to discern if an impression is from God is to realize that God will seldom give us impressions for someone else. When He does give us an impression it will NOT be for us to take a superior stance and proclaim, "Thus saith the Lord." Remember Job's friends were wrong about Job. There is always the possibility that we may be wrong about the origin of a thought, but God in His infinite mercy will correct us with patience if we come to Him honestly seeking to move on. I have found that God does often use other people to confirm a thought He has already given me.

Confirmation of a thought defined: clarification of a suspected leading of the Lord in our lives

Many of the thoughts we are given from God are tied to recognizing His providential will that proceeds behind the scenes to most people.

**** THE DIVINE PROVIDENCE OF GOD****

General providence refers to God's continuous upholding of the existence the natural order of the universe. He has an overarching plan for the ages. That plan involves us whether we know it or not.

Special providence refers to God's intervention in the lives of His people. We often miss this kind of leading because of God's subtle way of orchestrating events in our lives. He sees the past, present and future at the same time He gives us in life exactly what we need. It's hard for us to comprehend God's sovereign intelligence that surpasses our human intelligence by so much!

On the surface that seems true but the more a loving relationship grows the more we recognize Him. Like the two on the road to Emmaus our eyes are opened and we see Him working in our lives.

There are other words that describe His providence. A few of them are; provision, preparation of future events and needs, grace, guidance and supply. Luck is a word that should be struck from the list. Luck implies that we (the person) have a secret power that works to our advantage. It sounds strangely like superstition doesn't it? One thing is for sure God gets no praise or credit. The feel of His touch or the sensing of His Spirit is totally missing.

The more we recognize His participation in our lives the more grateful we become. When we follow the leading of our Lord, we will move beyond ourselves and find our calling and our destiny. As we follow Him we will cling to God, imitate Jesus, and pursue Him as The Way

For the child of God these so-called coincidences will increase when we are in His will. They can be like sigh post along the narrow way. Things we might have chalked up to good luck are now seen in a different light. The Light of His presence reveals the complexity of our relationship. But, I would add a word of caution. Jesus warned us about seeking signs. He told us not to do that. To this day I am surprised by the unexpected coordination of small events that He orchestrates as I keep my eyes on Him. His provision becomes a comfort and an encouragement. The gratitude that follows builds our faith like very few other things will.

THREE STORIES OF LOVE, INTERCESSION, DETERMINATION AND FAITH

There are several stories in the Bible about people who were paralyzed or so ill that they could not come to Jesus on their own initiative. We will look at two of those stories. The third is a parable about a woman who had to appeal to a man of authority for herself.

Each one teaches us about God's love and how we humans can intercede with determination and faith.

I would like to remind you of a story of four men who, unlike Job's "friends," were real friends to a man suffering physically and spiritually.

This story is found in the book of Luke. It has many important elements. I will delineate them for you.

Luke 5:18-25

Jesus is teaching in a house. The Scribes and Pharisees were in attendance. The home was so crowded that no one else could enter. The power of the Lord was present with Jesus to heal physical illness. There were a group of five men desperately desiring to attend the meeting. One of them was paralyzed. The able-bodied men were determined to present their friend to Jesus. It was Gods will for the man to be healed and He provided a way to complete the task at hand. The men saw clearly the obstacles before them, assessed the options and devised a providential plan. In those days houses usually had flat roofs comprised of a mat of branches and grass supported by wooden beams and covered with tiles. The men managed to get the paralyzed man on the roof, make an opening and lower him with his stretcher into the middle of the crowd and right in front of Jesus. When Jesus saw **their** **faith** in action springing from faith in Himself, He said, "Man your sins are forgiven." Then he said to him, "I say to you get up, pick up your stretcher and go home." He immediately stood up before them, picked up his stretcher, and went home glorifying and praising God."

The Pharisees began to think about the implications of the statement; "Your sins are forgiven." They determined that Jesus was speaking blasphemies by claiming to have the power to forgive sins. Jesus knowing the malice they held toward Him said, "Why are you questioning these things in your hostile thoughts? He answered them with another question, "Which is easier, to say, your sins are forgiven you, or to say, get up and walk?"

He was not at all intimidated by their position in the synagogue or their standing in the community. By the providence of God, Jesus was in the right place at the right time in order to display His deity. He was and He is the Son of God, the Messiah, and He has authority and power on earth to forgive sins.

All the elements of the story are worthy of our attention. But I want to focus on the intercessors and the healed man. Let's review. When He saw their faith in action the first thing He did was to address the man's spiritual problem; his sin. But notice this, it was the faith of all five that Jesus commended.

Like Jesus, they were not intimidated by the difficulties that presented themselves.

What are the precious truths we can extract to bless and encourage us today?

Just as the intercessors of that day, we are called to act as "go betweens" for another people. We have a choice. We can look on those paralyzed by a besetting sin and criticize them, or we can, as a labor of love, present them to God and pray that the "roof" or the barriers be broken. Those barriers may consist of many different habitual sins, addictions, pride or a distorted opinion of God in their minds. We all have immature places in us that need to be broken open so that healing can begin.

The man in the story came to Jesus and was rewarded but he needed help from his friends. They negotiated the physical difficulties, and they must have had a prayerful attitude, or they would not have been commended by Jesus for their faith. The man was not a passive participant. His obedience to Jesus command was a necessary element.

Intercessors defined: intermediaries, arbitrators, negotiators

Besetting sin defined: harassing, surrounding, assailing

As a child of God, we are commanded to examine
ourselves before we pray for others.

A STORY OF INTERCESSORY PRAYER

Our second story is about a Centurion who
intercedes for his slave who is dying.
Luke 7:1-10

The Centurion was a man who was in charge of one hundred men. He was a Gentile of wealth and influence. He was respected by Jews and Gentiles alike. His servant was gravely ill. But instead of going to Jesus himself or bringing the ill man to Jesus he sent two different groups of people to request Jesus heal the man. The first group he sent were Jewish elders. They made a request of Jesus. They said, "He is worthy for You to grant this to him; for he loves our nation, and it was he who built us our synagogue." (at this own expense)

As Jesus started to go to the slave the centurion sent friends (probably Gentiles) to repeat his words to Jesus saying, "Lord do not trouble Yourself further, for I am not worthy for You to come under my roof; therefore I did not even consider myself worthy to come to You, but just speak the word, and my servant will be healed. For I also am a man subject to authority, with soldiers under me; and I say to this one, "Go", and he goes, and to another, "Come," and he comes, and to my slave, "Do this," and he does it. Now when Jesus heard this, He was amazed at him, and turned and said to the crowd that was following Him, "I say to you, not even in Israel have I found such great faith [as this man's]" When the messengers who had been sent returned to the house, they found the slave in good health."

Jesus used the words "such great faith" to describe the Centurion because it pointed out a welcome contrast to the unbelief of the Jews.

The general opinion of Jews and Gentiles alike was that the Centurion had great worth. He himself knew better. Those who thought so highly of him, saw the fruit of his life and attributed the quality of his life to the man. But he was honest before God and man when he said, "I am not worthy."

This kind of wealth, power and influence can easily go to the head of the respected person and produce pride leading to selfishness and a lack of compassion for those around him. He did not fall into the trap of self-centeredness. He had a heart of compassion for a beloved servant and he had a sense of purpose. There is absolutely no mention of the servant pleading for help. He was gravely ill and could not make a request of Jesus for himself. The Centurion had a tender heart and a humble attitude. That attitude coupled with faith caused Jesus to marvel.

There is a saying, "I got nothin." There is more truth in those three words than volumes of books that have been written to try and convince us of our self-esteem (how much worth we have). When we get to the narrow gate, we will come with nothing. He realized he had nothing, and he realized that Jesus had everything. Again, contrast informs us of truth in a way nothing else could.

We see a model of community in action. A valiant warrior enlisted Jews and Gentiles to work together and communicate with Jesus for the benefit of someone unable to fend for himself. It sounds like intercession to me and a perfect picture of a man standing in the gap before God and for another man.

The atmosphere at this time between Jews and Gentile was very tense. Neither of them wanted a relationship with each other but the Father had a plan to breach the gap. His plan was for Jesus to break down the barrier between the two groups.

Ephesians 2:14 Paul said, "For He Himself is our peace and our bond of unity. He who made both groups- [Jews and Gentiles] – into one body and broke down the barrier, the dividing wall [of spiritual antagonism between us]. Amplified version

Remember the C.S. Lewis quote about this life being all about delegation? The centurion took orders from someone above him and he was a soldier in charge of one hundred men. Jesus commended him because he understood the concept of delegation and he had faith. It is unmistakable that all physical paralysis is not caused by sin. It is also clear that it is not God's will for all our infirmities to be healed this side of heaven. But the sin that paralyzes us spiritually need not be tolerated. Jesus is the Way, and He has made a way for us to be forgiven of our sins. He will direct us down the narrow path and keep our way straight into His arms.

THE THIRD STORY IS OF DETERMINATION
AND PERSISTANCE IN PRAYER – Luke 18:1-8

This parable is about the persistent widow and the unjust judge.

She appealed to a man who let his position of authority cause him to be callous toward a needy woman. Contrast him to the Centurion who also was similar in position of authority but very different in character.

"Now He (Jesus) was telling them a parable to show that at all times they ought to pray and not lose heart." Luke 18:1

He is encouraging all of us to not get discouraged because answers do not come immediately.

"There was in a certain city a judge who did not fear God and did not respect man." And there was a widow in that City, and she kept coming to him, saying, "Give me legal protection from my opponent."

"And for a while he was unwilling but afterward he said to himself, "Even though I do not fear god nor respect man, yet because this widow bothers me, **I will give her legal protection lest by continually coming she wear me out**." And the Lord said, "Hear what the unrighteous judge said; now shall not God bring about justice for His elect, who cry to Him day and night, and will He delay long over them? I tell you that He will bring about justice for them speedily. However, when the Son of Man comes, will He find faith on the earth? Luke 18:4-5

Speedily does not necessarily mean immediately. Since we do not know what the outcome will be curiosity and impatience can get the best of us.

Judges hold a position of respect in any society. And in any age, they have legal power to profoundly affect people's lives. That kind of authority can be very tiring. People are always wanting something. In this story the woman is at a marked disadvantage and easily taken for granted because women were not seen as equal to men and she had no husband to contend for her. The truth of the matter is that in Deuteronomy 11:18 widows and orphans are supposed to have special protection because of their vulnerable position. She loved God and she did not give in to self-pity. There are times when we may writhe in pain, but we must not wallow in it.

"At all times they ought to pray and not lose heart." Luke 18:1

> The inclination to trust God comes from Him.
> It comes with indignation and determination.
> It also comes with resolve to see "it" through
> and not let go even when, by our estimation,
> the answers to our prayers are delayed.

Constant Prayer

> It's a result of staying ever mindful of the Spirit's indwelling presence.
> Some prayers are as easy as breathing in and out.

"Rejoice always; pray without ceasing; in everything give thanks for this is God's will for you in Christ Jesus." 1 Thessalonians 5:16-18

Some Are Deliberate Daily Blessing Prayers

"The Lord is near to all who call upon Him, to ALL who call upon Him in truth." Psalm 145:18

Some Prayers Are Cries of Great Need

The woman in this parable had to engage in a process, plead for the judge to listen to her and help her. Jesus is telling us that we may have to wait until the time is right. The woman had to wait until the problem had progressed and a solution was received.

"The Lord is my portion," says my soul, "therefore I have hope in Him. The Lord is good to those who WAIT for Him, to the person who SEEKS Him. It is good that he waits silently for the salvation of the Lord." Lamentations 3:24-26

As I write the words of this chapter about intercessory prayer there are issues in my life that I am struggling with. There are requests that persist for years. As I write these words tears come to my eyes and my heart aches.

I Cannot Leave This Section of the Book Without Mentioning Fasting

FASTING defined: To voluntarily reduce or illuminate food for a time and for a specific purpose.

Fasting is mentioned in the Old and New Testaments. There are different kinds of Biblical fasts. The purpose is always to spend time praying and reading God's word. The yearning for food helps our spirit communicate with God as we turn our attention to Him. A very important exchange takes place. There can be a spiritual stronghold that needs to be broken through prayer and fasting. (see Luke 9:1-6) Perhaps there are specific insights He wants to give us but, the real reason for this special time will become evident as you actually do it!

Sometimes there is a desperate situation that calls for intense prayer that brings the person that is praying closer to God. Just like the tight rope walker has his eyes focused on a point ahead we must focus our attention on Jesus and not on our own efforts.

Several years ago I had fasted for a short time. I think it was for a day or two. At the end I said to the Lord, "Does this count?" His still small voice spoke to my spirit. He said, "I make it count." He comforted me with those words of encouragement. I was greatly relieved to know that my motivation had been submission to His will and not my human effort. No amount of straining and hand wringing will motivate Him to move on our behalf.

My Definition of FAITH

Instead of stressing out we rest assured that He hears us and will answer when He chooses and the way He chooses.

There are numerous references to fasting in the Bible but the one that cuts to the heart of the subject is Matthew 6:1-18. Jesus said, "When you give to the needy, when you pray and twice He said when you fast." He said "when." He did not say "If" you give, pray and fast. He clearly expects everyone to participate in some form or fashion.

Of course, fasting is not starvation, but the truth is that if I never ate again I would die. Food, water and the air we breath are our most basic necessities. Delaying food consumption is a reminder of how helpless we are. For the body, physical death is our ultimate humiliation. For the Christian it is the ultimate exaltation. In fasting we die to self.

"It is no longer I that live but Christ that lives within me." Galatians 2:20

As Christians we are "indwelt" by the Holy Spirit but to be under the power of the Spirit is different. To suspend or modify a behavior as basic as what you eat and when you eat gets down to that very important issue, Control!

Only in God's economy can our new birth arrange for that death to self that He requires. Of course, we can ignore His promptings, but sweet blessings await those who give, pray and fast.

Satan tests us to bring out the worst in us. God
tests us the bring out the best in us.
"Fasting test our faith and produces endurance. Humility
and endurance are a byproduct of fasting."
James 1:3 (My paraphrase)

The physical longing for food intensifies the longing for spiritual nourishment. After His conversation with the woman at the well, Jesus felt no need of food. He said, "My food is to do the will of My Father."

Lord, I come to You and I pray Hosanna save, Hosanna rescue. Show Yourself great and give me hope to never give up and never give in to despair. I realize that in every situation there are many elements that must fall into place before the answer is realized. Daniel waited 21 days than suddenly his answer came. Lord, do the work in me that needs to be done and send me down the narrow way. Amen

"The Lord is near to the broken hearted and saves those who are crushed in spirit. Many are the afflictions of the righteous; but the Lord delivers him out of them all." Psalm 34:18

He waits patiently for us to arrive in a place to receive His blessing and then He avenges us in His time and in His way.

So, what can we learn from an unjust judge who is not at all like our God Who is compassionate, just, and caring?

When God's will requires us to wait, we might begin to think of God as unjust. Nothing could be farther from the truth. We must not trust our lying emotions. How we respond to His will and His ways reveal a lot about us.

TIME IS THE GREAT REVEALER

It either reveals a broken spirit and a contrite heart
or time reveals an intact heart lacking sorrow over our own sin.
Time and time again He bids us come to Him.
With the bidding he gives the strength and power to come home.
Jesus is tenderly calling, "COME HOME – COME HOME."
He says, "All who are weary come home."

Don't forget it is Jesus Himself telling us the parable of the persistent widow. He teaches us through story telling because He knows we need to apply important truths to our lives. He created this scenario to instruct us to pray, pray, pray and never give up. He ends the parable with a question: "When the Son of Man returns will He find faith in the earth?"

Could it be that when good things happen in spite of sinful men and when against all odds our needs are met; God, not man, gets the glory? That realization will develop the faith on earth He desires. Our faith is perfected as we realize our weaknesses. When the Holy Spirit's power is added to our weaknesses, they become our strengths.

Our pride says that we should not have to suffer like this. If the world around us draws our focus away from Jesus the downward pull will drown us in self-pity.

Self-pity avoids true sorrow, hinders growth and keeps us from going deeper and lower with God.

GOD USES BROKEN THINGS

In the following section I want to add a brief review of the "broken" things mentioned in relation to the bible characters in this book.

"These things happened to them as an example.
But they were written down for our instruction." 1 Corinthians 10:11

Fellowship was broken when Adam and Eve sinned. In this fallen world brokenness is a part of living.

Jesus broke with tradition of the day and spoke to the Samaritan women. The two men on the road to Emmaus were broken hearted to hear Jesus had died. He took bread, blessed it and gave broken pieces to them. Their eyes were open. They recognized Him and He vanished from their sight. Jairus heart was broken to hear the news that his daughter had died. Jesus words spoke healing to him and His command to the daughter spoke physical healing to her. His words to Jairus daughter came with supernatural power to awaken her, body, soul and spirit. The older women had to be financially broken before she would reach out to Jesus. George Mueller was broken of the habit of being concerned about how he might serve in his public ministry. God did rid him of the notion that what he did publicly was more important than the private time they shared. God certainly did invite him to public ministry and together they accomplished many wonderful things. The "self" that felt nourished by good deeds was diminished and the "self" that allowed the Holy Spirit to nourish him was increased.

Nicodemus came to Jesus with words of flattery saying "Rabbi we know that you have come from God as a teacher; for no one can do these signs that You do unless God is with him." (John 3:2) As a scholar he should have known that Jesus was the long awaited Messiah but he didn't.

Jesus's response to him was to put Nicodemus in his place. Remember that place he puts us all in?

I think the questions Nicodemus asked revealed a man who was seeking information so that he could master it. What he got from Jesus was a lesson in transformation.

It is a foolish man that hears words, gathers information and stops there.
The wise man is one who hears and puts into practice
the words of God. It is the wise man that
allows God's word to master him.
Transformation is about who we are becoming
and what we do as a result of it.

We do know that Nicodemus was accepting of the truth Jesus spoke to him because of actions he took surrounding Jesus death, burial and resurrection.

God's laws show us that there is such a thing as right and wrong. It is revelatory. When we break the laws of the Bible, and we will, our need of the Savior is amplified. The law serves the purpose of declaring that there is a Higher Power and that when the pressures of life close in on us we realize that we are in desperate need of the Savior. He also breaks us of thinking we are capable of cleaning up our sinful selves. The "self" we construct will have to be broken and remolded like the clay in the potter's hands. Worship of God based on His provision breaks the cycle of bondage to sin and slavery is replaced by the spirit of adoption as sons and daughters. Along with the family inheritance comes wisdom to judge evil properly. In the process we will be broken of the habit of unjustly criticizing other people for falling short of a standard we have established. The law, without Gods love at the center, is like stagnant water. It seems like it might satisfy, but the truth is Jesus offers us rivers of living water. He will use the world, our flesh and the devil to break the ground of our hardened heart and clear the path for the Holy Spirit's precious presence so that the fruit of his Spirit can flourish. In the process He will break us of the idea that we must clean ourselves up and pretend to be someone we are not. Our true identity will emerge as we take our eyes off ourselves and focus on the Savior. He will break the idea that temptation is sin, and the habit of constantly comparing ourselves with other people. We will stop needing to be reassured of our identity. In the abiding state our true calling will emerge.

From our perspective Jesus broke the laws of nature to heal the sick and revive the dead. They are His laws and subject to His Sovereignty. He can do whatever He pleases. These "laws" of nature are His design, and He is perfectly within His rights to use them any way He chooses to bring about His will. In the process He will break our contract state of mind and enlighten our path to rest in His covenant.

Mary and Martha knew quite well that Jesus was willing and able to heal the sick. He had already been doing that for a while by the time Lazarus fell ill. What they failed to take into account is the idea that Jesus was not independent of the Father or the Holy Spirit. They work together and have reasons for things They do or do not do. Those things go far beyond anything we could ask or think.

Their family unit was shattered when Lazarus died but when he came alive again their broken hearts where mended.

The Father broke the prodigal son's stubborn self-will by allowing him to choose to openly rebel. The rebellion revealed his true condition and served to bless him with a broken spirit and a contrite heart.

"My sacrifice, O God, is a broken spirit; a broken and contrite heart you, God will not despise." Ps. 51:17

In Jesus parable the son's disposition needed a course correction. The way he looked at life was a weapon Satan used to try to ruin his life. God used it to break his stubborn self-will. Gratitude toward his father gave him freedom to come home.

There is no action we can take, no work or behavior that will satisfy God except a willingness to accept our brokenness and allow His forgiveness to bring healing. That sacrifice is acceptable and worthy of reward.

The process of relinquishing control of our lives and embracing God's proper place puts us in touch with Reality. He knows that gratitude to God produces a blessed life. The heavenly Father takes what we prodigal children give Him. He uses our rebellion to break us of our selfish desires. In his spiritual darkness the prodigal son thought worldly pleasure would satisfy the longing of his heart. He was pressed into knowing no helper but God and pressed into loving the staff and the rod.

"All of us like sheep have gone astray. Each of us has turned to his own way." Isaiah 53:6

Psalm 23:4 "Thy rod and Thy staff they comfort me."

God, in His wisdom, knows that the written Word of God is our refuge in time of uncertainty and trouble. He uses the written word to correct our behavior by bringing conviction of our sin.

> Shepherds use the rod to protect sheep from danger and to correct their behavior. The rod is like an extension of His own arm. It symbolized His authority, power and His strength. When a sheep was determined to wander away the rod becomes a tool of correction. When the shepherd saw a sheep about to wander away or getting close to danger he would with skill send the rod flying through the air. The stubborn animal would then hurry back to the flock. The staff was used to comfort the sheep and encourage them to stay together. He used the crooked end to pull an individual sheep close to himself or guide them down his chosen path.

The precious Holy Spirit is our comforter in times of trouble and He guides us down the path and through the narrow gate marked, "Only Forgiven Sinners Enter Heaven Here." He says to our spirit; "this is the way walk in it."

The Heavenly Father used Satan's attacks to bless Job and everyone who reads the account of his life. Job had to be broken of the notion that God should consult him about the affairs of this world. Job's virtuous life was not in question. God permitted his life to be shattered and then used the shattered pieces to reveal precious truths he could have not learned any other way.

Jeremiah repented of his impatience and God's blessing flowed through his loneliness. He experienced broken relationships because God had called him to deliver warnings of judgement that people did not like. The people of Jeremiah's day were rigid in their heart's desires. The judgement that

Jeremiah warned them about did happen because they refused to be broken of their sinful ways and repent.

Job and Jeremiah suffered loss and experienced pain we cannot even imagine. He tested their characters and, in the process, revealed His own character. The reassurance He gives us in the midst of our problems breaks us of thinking our troubles are God's way of punishing us because He is angry and vengeful toward His own.

Even when God did send judgement, as a result of David's sin, His purpose was to set things right and bless His people with a king after His own heart. King David's sinful census had consequences. He was warned by God's prophet, but he proceeded to count his soldiers anyway. David had to be broken of acting foolishly and making decisions without praying first.

The story of Gideon stands in stark contrast to David's story. They both came to the same conclusion but in very different ways. They were both afraid of the enemy just beyond their border. The contrast was evident in the outcome of the story.

Gideon was worried. He was bothered by the cares of the world. He was anxious and uneasy about their enemies the Midianites. In spite of his fear, God declared him a Valiant Warrior. Gideon was used by God to break down and destroy the alter of Baal. Gideon means "the destroyer." His new name was Jerubbaal which means let Baal contend against Him. God used him to break everyone's idea that more soldiers are better than a few soldiers chosen by God. They broke pitchers to reveal the light that was hidden for a time. We are like that pottery. Our purpose is hidden until the time is right. When God calls us to reveal His presence then the darkness is dispatched. The enemy is confused and victory is ours. He had almost let his emotions get the best of him, but he resisted his spiritual enemy who would love to enslave him to his fear. And guess what? His emotions fell in line with God's order for things, God's plan was revealed, and God won the battle for him.

"Do not be afraid and do not be dismayed at this great horde for the battle is not yours but Gods." 2Chronicles 20:15b

"One man of you puts to flight a thousand, since it is the Lord your God who fights a thousand, since it is the Lord God who fights for you, just as He promised you." Joshua 23:10

The intercessors broke through the roof to lower the paralyzed man to Jesus. They negotiated a physically difficult situation. Today's intercessors have authority to pray for their fellow mankind. As spiritual intercessors we are called to be intermediaries between God and man. We have the privilege of standing in that gap. When the necessary brokenness does happen, we can see the providence of God in their lives.

The Centurion broke the idea of what "worthiness" really was when He rightly evaluated his position in society. His humility in the face of the admiration of men was a marvel even to the Lord.

In the parable of the persistent widow God describes a process that breaks us of our impatience to see justice for an unjust act. We are reminded to not give up when, by our estimation, God's will is delayed by people who think they are in control.

Jesus and the Father have <u>unbroken</u> fellowship.

The desire of God's heart is to have unbroken fellowship with us.

Remember His words to His beloved people in Moses time.

"Oh that they had such a heart in them, that they would fear Me and keep all My commandments always, that it may be well with them and with their sons forever. "

In the New Testament John spoke these words.

"And we have come to know and have believed the love which God has for us. God is love, and the one who abides in love abides in God, and God abides in him." 1 John 4:16

The abiding life is usually defined as "remaining" consciously aware of His presence. It is a correct term but not enough to fully cover the meaning of the word. Without further explanation it could imply a motionless existence. Abiding can also be defined by the following terms: joyfulness, willingness to be pruned, willingness to follow God, obedience minded, soft hearted, exhorted, comforted, strengthened, in touch with Reality, encouraged, the realization of never being alone and unbroken fellowship.

Intercession of the Son of God for His Loved Ones

See John 17:1-26 to read entire prayer passage.

Jesus offered prayer for His own glorification, believers protection, sanctification, and the mission of the church to send the gospel of Jesus Christ into the world. He declares His desire to spend eternity with His loved ones and He intercedes for those who will form the church.

The following are selected portions: John 17: 1-3, 11B, 15-17, 22, 26

These things Jesus spoke and lifting up His eyes to heaven, He said, "Father, the hour had come, glorify Thy Son, that the Son may glorified Thee, even as Thou gavest Him authority over all mankind, that to all whom Thou hast given Him, He may give eternal life. . . . "And this is eternal life, that they may know Thee, the only true God, and Jesus Christ whom Thou hast sent. . . ." I come to Thee Holy Father, keep them in Thy name, the name which thou hast given Me, that they may be one, even as We are. . . I do not ask Thee to take them out of the world, but to keep them from the evil one. "They are not of the world, even as I am not of the world. "Sanctify them in the truth; Thy word is truth. . . . "And the glory which Thou hast given Me I have given to them; that they may be one just as We are one; . . . and I have made Thy name known to them, and will make it known; that the love wherewith Thou didst love Me may be in them, and I in them."

Adam and Eve had no separation from God in the Garden before the fall of man. Our loss began then and there. Redemption is the reversal of that loss. It makes it possible for us to come home in prayer for now and with completion in heaven for eternity.

Remember, the trinity of Father, Son, and Holy Spirit have unbroken fellowship. It will not be like that for us until we are with Them in heaven. 1 John 3:2

> "Come to Me, all you that are weary and heavy-
> laden, and I will give you rest."
> Take My yoke upon you, and learn from Me,
> for I am gentle and humble in heart.
> and you shall find rest for your souls." Matthew 11:28

Dear Lord, we need You every moment of every day. The sin that entangles us serves to reveal how much we need You. That sin can hinder our ability to come home from the far country of our own making. The process all begins with Your call "Come to Me." And it ends with the response of an honest seeking heart, "Yes Lord, I come . . . I come! Amen

NOTES

Chapter 1: The Day That Changed My Life

Chapter 2: Innocence Lost – Innocence Shattered

1. Hymn: Victory In Jesus lyrics by Eugene Bartlett
2. Hymn: Precious Memories lyrics, author J.B.F. Wright
3. Taken from My Utmost for His Highest(R) by Oswald Chambers, Copyright © 1935 by Dodd Mead & Co., renewed © 1963 by the Oswald Chambers Publications Assn., Ltd. Used by permission of Our Daily Bread Publishing, Grand Rapids, MI 49501. All rights reserved. "The springs of love are in God, not in us. It is absurd to look for the love of God in our hearts naturally, it is only there when it has been shed abroad in our hearts by the Holy Spirit."
4. Quote: Thomas Manton 1920-1677 (Public domain)
5. Taken from The Complete Works of Oswald Chambers, Copyright © 2000 by the Oswald Chambers Publications Association, Limited. Used by permission of Our Daily Bread Publishing, Grand Rapids, MI 49501 All rights reserved.
6. C.S. Lewis quote, "We wonder not that God has our best in mind. We wonder how painful His best will turn out to be."

Chapter 3: Let Go and Let God

1. Hymn, Bring Ye All The Tithes Into The Storehouse "Trust Me Try Me" author Lida Leech (died 1962)
2. Martin Luther quote "God created the world out of nothing. If we remember that we are nothing then God can make something out of us." (Public Domain)

Chapter 4: Our True Purpose

1. David Wilkerson, quote from his Pulpit Series Newsletter dated Feb. 13,2002
2. C.S. Lewis, prayer for the lost "Lord keep on loving them till you love them into loving you."

Chapter 5: Two More Honest Seeking Hearts

1. Oswald Chambers, My Utmost for His Highest (October 12th devotion) page 286 Dodd Mead & Co., renewed © 1963 by the Oswald Chambers Publications Assn. Ltd. Used by permission of Our Daily bread Publishing, Grand Rapids, MI 49501. All rights reserved. "The worth of a man is revealed in his attitude to ordinary things when he is not before the footlights."

Chapter 6: The Story of the Two Daughters

1. Chorus, I Will Change our Name (author unknown)
2. Dan Allender, Ph. D., The Healing Path-Commentary on Mathew (Water Brook Press, 12265 Oracle Blvd. Suite 200, Colorado Springs, Colorado 80921) page *****

Chapter 7: Relax – Relate – Rely – Relinquish Control

1. Hymn: What a Friend We Have in Jesus, Lyrics by Joseph M. Scriven published 1865
2. Autobiography of George Muller comp. Fred Bergen (London:j. Nisvet. 1906) 152-4

Chapter 8: My "Testimony" In A Court of Law

Chapter 9: Hinderances to Fellowship with Our Lord – Misplaces Fears

1. Michael Wells, Sidetracked in the Wilderness, Published by Abiding Life Press a division of Abiding Life Ministries International PO

Box 620998, Littleton CO 80162 Quote: "My only responsibility is to abide. Everything else makes life difficult."

2. M. Scott Peck quote
3. Annie Johnson Flint, Pressure Poem (Annie died 1932)
4. C.S. Lewis, quote: "The prayer that proceeds all other prayer is, may the real me meet the real you."
5. Michael Wells, Sidetracked in the Wilderness, Published by Abiding Life Press a division of Abiding Life Ministries International PO Box 620998, Littleton, CO 80162 Quote: "Are you certain you want to be free? If you want to be free pray this prayer. Lord, apart from You I can do nothing; today I give You _____, and I thank YOU that no matter what, You have taken it. What is needed is the supernatural action of God that comes only when we have our eyes off the problem and on Him through abiding."
6. Michael Wells, Sidetracked in the Wilderness, Published by Abiding Life Press a division of Abiding Life Ministries International PO Box 620998, Littleton, CO 80162 Quote: "He only permits wounding that accelerates our ending well. And He only prevents things that would hinder that same ending."
7. Scripture taken from The Message. Copyright © 1993, 1994,1995 1996,2000,2001,2002. Used by permission of NavPress Publishing Group. (Psalm 119:71-72)
8. George Mc Donald quote: "Few delights equal the mere presence of One we trust utterly"

Chapter 10: Misconceptions of Who God Really Is

1. Charles Hadden Spurgeon quote: "Nothing happens to us that we would not wish for ourselves if we were as wise and loving as God."
2. A.W. Tozer, The Next Chapter After the Last
3. Answered Prayer Poem, author unknown
4. GUIDANCE poem – author unknown
5. Oswald Chambers, My Utmost for His Highest * by Oswald Chambers, Copyright © 1935 by Dodd Mead & Co., renewed © 1963 by Oswald Chambers Publications Assn., Ltd. Used by

permission of Our Daily Bread Publishing, Grand Rapids, MI 49501. All rights reserved. "Getting into the stride of God means nothing less than union with Himself. It takes a long time to get there, but keep at it. Don't give in because the pain is bad just now, get on with it, and before long you will find you have a new vision and a new purpose."

Chapter 11: Our Stubborn Self Will

1. Michael Wells, Sidetracked in the Wilderness, Published by Abiding Life Press a division of Abiding Life Ministries International PO Box 620998, Littleton CO 80162 Quote: "You don't know that Jesus is all you need until Jesus is all you've got."
2. Kathy Freeburg quote: "Emotions are the best of servants and the worst of masters."
3. The Message Eugen Peterson, Copyright © 1993,1994,1995,199 6,200,2001,2002. quote, "God gets down on His knees among us . . . gets on our level and shares Himself with us. He does not reside afar off and send diplomatic messages, He kneels down among us . . . God shares Himself generously and graciously."

Chapter 12: Our God is Triune, The Great Three In One

1. Taken from My Utmost for His Highest ® by Oswald Chambers, Copyright © 1935 by Dodd Mead & Co., renewed © 1963 by the Oswald Chambers Publications Assn., Ltd. Used by permission of Our Daily Bread Publishing, Grand Rapids, MI 49501 All rights reserved.) "Men will not wait for the slow, steady way of God;)

Chapter 13: The Stories of Job and Jeremiah

1. Scripture taken from The Message Copyright © 1993,1994,1995,1 996,2000,2001,2002. Used by permission of NavPress Publishing Group. (Mark 4:9) Metaphor of soil for ears.

Chapter 14: The Masters Plan for Our Lives

1. George Hodges, The Purpose of Trouble quote by George Hodges. (1856-1919) He was an American Episcopal theologian born at Rome, New York and educated at Hamilton College. He wrote 62 books. His most popular book is <u>The Early Church: From Ignatius to Augustine</u>.
2. Phillip Keller, A Shepherd Looks at the 23rd Psalm Page 69

Chapter 15: Prayer, Our Holy Occupation

1. Taken from My Upmost for His Highest ® by Oswald Chambers, Copyright © 1935 by Dodd Mead & Co., renewed © 1963 by the Oswald Chambers Publications Assn., Ltd.. Used by permission of Our Daily bread Publishing, Grand Rapids, MI 49501. All rights reserved.
2. Dan Allender, The Healing Path, page 37
3. Michael Wells, Sidetracked In the Wilderness, Published by Abiding Life Press a division of Abiding Life Ministries International PO Box 620998, Littleton, CO 80162 Quote: "In His presence and by His power, the ten commandments become the ten promises; that we will not commit those sins."
4. Sylvia Gunter and Arthur Burk, Blessing Your Spirit,

Chapter 16: The Straight and Narrow Way

1. Michael Wells, Sidetracked In the Wilderness, published by Abiding Life Press a division of Abiding Life International PO Box 620998, Littleton, CO 80162 quote: "In every situation there are many facts we have no way of knowing."

Printed in the United States
by Baker & Taylor Publisher Services